**THE MODERN SOUL**
**INDIGENOUS WISDOM**
**THE JUNGIAN PROJECT**

# WAY AHEAD

## Medicine Stories

For permission requests, write to the publisher, addressed "Attention: Permissions Coordinator," at the address below.
Bloom Factor Press
4115 Glencoe Avenue, Suite 105
Marina del Rey, CA 90292
www.BloomFactorPress.com

Ordering Information:
Quantity sales. Special expanded wholesale availability is available on quantity purchases by corporations, associations, academic libraries and others. For details, contact the publisher CreateSpace >>> www.createspace.com/pub/l/createspacedirect.do or order the book, workbook and journal through one of the regular wholesalers, e.g., Ingram.

ISBN-10: 1986064506
ISBN-13: 978-1986064507
Library of Congress In-Publication Data
Glock Ph.D. Michael
**Way Ahead — Medicine Stories**
1. Jungian Psychology 2. Futuristics 3. Applied Psychology
Project authored and designed by Michael Glock Ph.D.
Front & Back cover photograph by Photo by Michael Carnevale on Unsplash
Interior typeset in Oswald (chapter headings) Sabon (body) and Montserrat (callout's). Front & back cover set in Gobold and Neuton.

Printed in the United States of America
Published by Bloom Factor Press
www.blooomfactorpress.com
Second printing – February 2018
302928272625242322212019181716151413121110987654321

# Disclaimer

This book is not intended as a substitute for Analytical Psychology, it does not offer a complete framework. It is not a substitute for Jungian Analysis or other forms of psychoanalysis or psychotherapy. The reader should regularly consult a physician in matters relating to his/her mental health and particularly with respect to any symptoms, physical and or psychological that may require attention, diagnosis, therapy or analysis. Some names and identifying details have been changed to protect the privacy of individuals.

# Early International Acclaim

Way Ahead is a brilliant flagship of depth psychology, helping us to steer through our present global chaos and cross road disenchantments. Through his own vibrant scholarship and world wide venturing Michael introduces the profound work of Jung and post Jungians, engaging with the paradoxes of our clamoring human needs, weaving our journey into world wide myths and cultures, threading the wisdom of ancient mystery schools with contemporary finds in neuroscience and quantum physics. Most significantly Michael provides us with concrete tools to distinguish between our personal and collective hubristic fantasies – a shadow side of creation - and our potent, dreams and embodied imagination that can lead us into deeper fulfillment and a capacity for sustained commitment to healing and enriching communities.

*~ Dr. Evangeline Rand. Registered Psychologist, Edmonton, Canada*

Michael Glock has written a unique and creative approach to design thinking with Way Ahead. With a conceptual design system focused on Jungian and Apache theories and praxis, the framework tackles life's obstacles for a deeper understanding of who you are and what you want from life. This is not simply self-improvement, but a destiny design system that can influence your thinking about how to weigh and make the choices you need for more satisfying living. Glock's unique background offers depth and insight into Futuristics and how to combine this with contemporary design thinking, a necessary treatise for the ills of our day.

*~ Stephani Stephens, PhD, Independent Scholar, Canberra, Australia.*

Boldly reaching across time in a trans-historical manner, as he trans-Culturally links diverse cultures and traditions into a single vision, in this ground-breaking work, Michael Glock widens the scope of our perspectives on the confluences of past, present and future, the inner worlds of psychic reality, including the spiritual realms, with the outer ones of everyday external realities resulting in a re-enchantment of the diverse visions in a way that promotes continuing intersubjective dialogues. This book truly fulfils the author's dream of writing 'a book that inspires readers to understand, heal and upgrade their lives.'

~ *Dr. Gottfried M. Heuer, Jungian Psychoanalyst, author of Freud's 'Outstanding' Colleague/Jung's 'Twin Brother: Otto Gross (Routledge, 2017). Book discussion with Jonathan Chadwick https://vimeo.com/196609212 London, United Kingdom.*

"I have read and enjoyed reading Way Ahead very much, particularly about Michael Glock's background in New Zealand. It's an uplifting, joyous work which will help those people who have lost their bearing in life to find a new way forward."

~ *Dr. phil. Elizabeth Brodersen, Jungian Training Analyst, CGJI Zürich, Switzerland & Franfurt, Germany.*

"This is a wonderful book for all of us who are searching for greater direction, purpose and meaning in our inner and outer lives and the required congruence between the two. I highly recommend it."

~ *Rabbi Stan Levy, Counsel Manatt, Phelps & Phillips, LLP. Los Angeles, California ,USA.*

"I was moved because I see how Michael has struggled to seek his own soul. It is a difficult journey. It has touched me deeply. He is showing the way for young people to find their way while being beautifully grounded in Jungian psychology.

In Japanese culture, it is amazing that most young people do not feel conflicted even though their social situation is radically hopeless. They delve into and devote themselves to SNS, idols, anime's and create relationships in small groups to avoid their real crisis. Way Ahead is a way out and through for them."

*~ Konoyu Nakamura, PhD. Professor for clinical psychology at Otemon Gakuin University, Osaka, Japan, Jungian oriented psychotherapist, Member of EC of IAJS. Tokyo, Japan.*

"Michael accomplishes many things in this book. Not only does he succeed in telling a good story, one that is compelling and requires that we turn to the next page to see what happens next but, he also conveys significant meaning in a straight forward manner. This balancing is especially important for communicating the depth psychological work of C.G. Jung.

Many of us have spent years studying Jung's many complex meanings and our efforts have deepened and extended Jung's work. The project that Michael has taken on and succeeded at, that few others have done as well, is taking our complexity and communicating it in a friendly and welcoming language."

*~ Peter T. Dunlap PhD, Analyst in private practice. Author of **Awakening Our Faith in the Future: the Advent of Psychological Liberalism.** Published by Routledge London, England. California, USA.*

"Captivating and clear, Way Ahead entices its readers into a way of self-contemplation that engages more than consciousness and ego but rather lures out the facets of the full personality. Using classic stories and precepts of Jungian depth psychology, Michael Glock recounts his personal journey in ways that make it a universal quest, with short exercises to bring it home. A warm and confident voice, Glock's book touches us all."

~ *Leslie Gardner, Fellow, Centre for Psychoanalytic Studies, University of Essex, co-editor 'Feminist Views from Somewhere' with Fran Gray (Routledge 2016). London, United Kingdom.*

"Authentic, engaging, useful - Way Ahead by Michael Glock is an invitation to imagine, intuit and actualize our destinies using Jungian psychology, scientific reasoning, inner attitude and journaling. Michael invites readers to travel into their inner lives and rebuild their destinies, while he effortlessly takes us through Jungian concepts, world myths and stories of life in multiple cultures and continents. From an Indian perspective, this practical handbook can be of immense help to people experiencing life-transitions, as conceived in the ancient Indian concept of the four stages of life, where every transition can be seen as a symbolic rebirth, and as Michael so deftly shows in this book, a Way Ahead way to renew oneself by throwing open the gates to the future."

~ *Sulagna Sengupta, M.A., Member, India Jung Centre, Bangalore, India; Author, 'Jung in India', Spring Journal Books, USA. Bangalore, India.*

"Targeting the self-help book market, Michael Glock's Way Ahead is a very accessible, smart, and timely introduction to the significance of post-Jungian concepts in the twenty-first century. Anyone wishing to lead a happier, more fulfilling yet grounded life will finish this book pondering the Probable, Preferable, and Possible and then feel ready to take the first step towards self-realization."

~ *Jutta Schamp, Ph.D. College Lecturer at California State Universities, Dominguez Hills and Northridge; Santa Monica College. California, USA.*

# Acknowledgement

John Archibald Wheeler (1911-2008) was a visionary physicist who said "May the universe in some strange sense be brought into being by those that participate".

This statement and teaching style inspired me when I immigrated to the United States decades ago. Professor Wheeler was a quantum physicist, a field with far reaching implications regarding the way we understand the hidden dimension of our inner psychological realm and the sub atomic world of physics. Years ago I printed out those words on little cards and placed them throughout my house and glued them onto the mirror in the bathroom so I would be reminded daily of the necessity to participate.

A deep thank you goes to my wife Rochelle, who continues to love and support my medicine work. Thank you to my mother and father Susie and Ernst Glock; Susie, I did become a philosopher! Special thank you to my grandmother Oma Boba who taught me Russian and how to cook Red Borscht and Kasha and how to care for the soul.

Thank you goes to all my teachers, especially Robert Romanyshyn, Mary & Ron Hulnick & Elana Golden, my book editor and creative consultant, who was able to take my clever but disparate philosophies and mash-ups and turn them into a cohesive story with an excellent launch, a concrete interior and impeccable culmination.

Thank you to all the mentors, teachers, philosophers, men's group members, therapists, International Association for Jungian Studies (IAJS) committee members, Jungian colleagues, and all the one-time UBER and Lyft conversations. You've all contributed to my progress. This journey has been, by way of Yale and Cornell Universities, Arizona State University, Boston University, in the United States, the ETH in Zurich, Switzerland and the University of Greenwich in London and the Center for the Book in Cape Town, South Africa

Infinite thanks to the flora and fauna of New Zealand—Land of the Long White cloud, to the dreamtime in Australia, German engineering, the culinary delights of France and Italy, the sand gardens of Japan, and the island magic of Moorea.

Thank you, Earth.

# CONTENTS

# Figures

INTRODUCTION
# STORY AND SOUL

*"Storytelling may have been the earliest art form. It is an essential means of individual and social expression common to all peoples. Every culture has evolved a framework of stories to describe and to reconcile the complementary worlds of reality and imagination. Far more than simple entertainment, the stories represent the cultural memory and imaginative history of the community. They encode the values considered important for survival. Both the commonplace and the important events of life are understood in relation to these stories and the beliefs they express."*

**From: The Inuit Imagination, a work on the art and stories of the Inuit peoples of the far North.**

Way Ahead is based on the Jungian project. Jungian Culture has similar stories to those of the Inuit people; their function is to draw together the worlds of reality and the imagination, and help reconcile the complimentary worlds of our everyday ego consciousness and our fantasies that have deep roots in the unconscious. Reality offers us, individually and collectively, many pleasures and satisfactions, and also confronts us with severe challenges. Imagination offers a way to escape and enjoy, and to engage in reality with all its multiplicity, from positive to negative aspects. Stories combine the two realms ingeniously and act as symbols, drawing wisdom from the deep well of the unconscious. These are the machineries of existence that we hurl ourselves into when working the Way Ahead system.

Imagination and reality must meet and touch one another, intertwine, and form a magical, mystical marriage of the opposites—to bear fruit. A symbolic story is the child of lived experience and interpenetration. We need such stories to guide us in our work. We need stories to live by. We draw wisdom from the wellspring of dreams, which combine features of reality and dynamic, often dramatic, elements of the imagination. And so, our symbolic story becomes the mother and father of our new life.

Carl G. Jung has bequeathed us a wonderful story of this kind to draw upon as a community. He received it from his friend, Richard Wilhelm. I'm speaking of the "Rainmaker Story." It is by now woven deeply into Jungian Culture, and so I bring it to you here in this book—to receive it in the context of destiny design.

There was a great drought where Wilhelm lived in China: for months there had not been a drop of rain and the situation became catastrophic. The Catholics made processions, the Protestants made prayers, and the Chinese burned joss sticks and shot off guns to frighten away the demons of the drought, but with no result. Finally the village's elder said: we will fetch the rainmaker. And from another province, a dried up old man appeared.

The only thing the old man asked for was a quiet little house somewhere, and there he locked himself in for three days. On the fourth day clouds gathered, unleashing a great snowstorm at a time of the year when no snow was ever expected. The village was so full of rumors about the wonderful rainmaker that Wilhelm went to him to ask how he had done it. In true European fashion Wilhelm said:

"They call you the rainmaker, will you tell me how you made the snow?"

The elderly Chinese man said: "I did not make the snow, I am not responsible." "But what have you done these three days?"

"Oh, I can explain that. I come from another province where things are in order. Here they are out of order, they are not as they should be by the ordnance of Heaven. Therefore the whole country is not in Tao, and I am also not in the natural order of things because I am in a disordered province. So I had to wait three days until I was back in Tao, and then naturally the rain and the snow came."

This story, like so many symbolic tales, tempts us to ask: is it really true? Did that really happen once upon a time in Qingdao, China? However, we also know that when we deal with symbolic stories, as with dreams and fantasies, it is forbidden to ask this true-or-false question. The story exists in an intermediate realm of the psyche. To inject the one-sided "reality" question here would fracture the marriage between fact and the imagination and destroy their child, the symbolic story.

So we hold the story in our hands like an ancient and fragile Ming vase, and gently inquire into its meanings. There are many. The story offers us points of wisdom reflected from the depths, which we may meditate upon and try to understand for the purpose of designing our future in alignment with the Tao.

So what does this story tell you as you move on towards the future if we take it as a symbol—a statement of psychic truth?

The first thing the Rainmaker Story tells me is this: there are problems in life where external solutions are not effective. Here we find a province locked in drought, a dire condition. Without water, life itself is threatened and new life is therefore impossible. A drought can be seen as a symbol for being trapped by the stories of our past, "I can't do this or that because I..." The land of consciousness is cut off from the sources of life- giving-waters that reside in the unconscious. It is a wasteland. We know this problem well, as we have all experienced it and came to recognize it as blocked access to the energies that drive us forward. The future is to be found in the living waters of the unconscious—the heavens of Spirit and the underworld of our instincts and impulses. You can't solve your life's problems with conventional means because they do not connect to the sources of life. The province is out of Tao, out of balance.

For the most part, rituals have become nothing more than occasions for noise-making and traditional prayers no more than exercises for the vocal chords. People try everything but the beneficial—jogging, pill popping, going to the movies, shopping—all of these activities are usually nothing but distractions without a lasting positive effect. Yet, this is what we live in and paradoxically what life journeys are often made of—polluted, muddy waters. None offers a long-term sustainable solution to this problem of inner draught. I know too that frequently advice, assignments, exercises, diagnoses and whatever else are unworkable because they do not contact the unconscious source, the living waters. This is why Way Ahead is structured as a workbook; it is a way to discover and release the life force of the healing, living waters within you.

*Figure 1: Inukshuk at Wreck Beach Vancouver Canada.*

## CHAPTER ONE
# THE CROSSROADS

*"The Seeker. This archetype refers to one who searches on a path that may begin with earthly curiosity but has at its core the search for God and/or enlightenment. Unlike the Mystic, which has the Divine as its sole focus, the Seeker is in search of wisdom and truth wherever it is to be found. The shadow side of the archetype is the "lost soul," someone on an aimless journey without direction, ungrounded, disconnected from goals and others."*

*~ Carolyn Myss*

n 2002 I was at a crossroads in my life—I was successful yet strangely empty. I was disinterested in individuals and had no close family or thicket of engagements. I kept thinking of Oedipus, the mythical Greek hero in Sophocles' tragedy Oedipus the King, for the story gave voice to my own questioning about the mystery of human life.

In Sophocles' play, a prophecy foretold that the king and queen of Thebes would give birth to a son who would kill his father and marry his mother.

When their son, Oedipus, is born, the king leaves him to die on a mountainside in order to thwart the tragic prophecy. But the baby is found and raised by shepherds, and later, as s young man, Oedipus bids farewell to the countryside and heads for Thebes, the big city. On the way, at a crossroads, he meets an older man, and not knowing it is his father he fights him and kills him.

Arriving in Thebes, Oedipus finds the city's citizens in mourning for the recent murder of their king. A riddle is circulated at the gate to the city, and he who would solve it is promised the throne to the kingdom. Oedipus defeats all other contestants in solving the riddle and wins the throne of the dead king, and the hand in marriage of the king's widow—who is his mother. Thus the prophecy has been fulfilled. The Chorus cries out: "Even Oedipus, greatest of men, was brought low by destiny, for he unknowingly murdered his father and married his mother." When Oedipus learns the truth he blinds himself and exiles himself from the city of Thebes.

At the end of the play order is restored when his uncle becomes king, and complying with Oedipus' request promises to take care of Oedipus' children. But Oedipus's children would always bear the weight of shame and humiliation because of their father's actions.

The tragic fate of Oedipus intrigued me and echoed my questions. What is fate? What is destiny? What is prophecy and what determines its fulfillment? Can the future be known? Who, what, creates the future? These queries do not have a definite answer. In her book Writing for Your Life, writer and philosopher Deena Metzger writes, "There is no solution, for example, to the fate of King Lear or Oedipus; to look for one is to reduce great works of art to the trivialities of pop psychology. Such works speak to the paradoxes and dilemmas of the human condition, even as the questions we ask take us ever more deeply into the eternal dilemma." Such works of art illumine and inspire our questioning and contemplation; they are the diving boards into the depth of our own psyches.

But one thing however, in the tragic Oedipus the King play, seemed clear to me: that which is kept secret, disowned, and hidden in the unconscious will eventually find its way out into the light of day. Often this "eruption of truth" happens at the crossroads, sometimes the set of horror, and always at a high price.

*Figure 2: On the West Coast Road. From the album: N.Z. Scenery, 1879, Dunedin,*

Since my teenage years, hiking the land in New Zealand, I had been attracted to psychology, philosophy, to the wisdom of the mind and the magic of Spirit. My quest took me from the encounter groups of the 1970s and 80s that encouraged defiance of social restrictions and open, honest interactions with others, to Shamanic trainings and initiations, to rites of passage ceremonies using Ayahuasca—a brew that produces spiritual revelations about the nature of life, the universe, and one's psyche. My quest ultimately brought me to the study of Tantra—an ancient Indian tradition of meditation and ritual that channels the divine energy of the macrocosm into the human sexual microcosm—and to the Men's Consciousness movement led by activist and author Robert Bly. It is through Robert that I came to know and become inspired by such great poets of our time as Pablo Neruda and Antonio Machado, and Rumi, Hafez, Kabir and Mirabai of times past.

Yet all of this searching seemed random. I was hungry, but for what? I remember always thinking that I would not fight for King or Country; I would fight for humanity, I would fight for racial and gender equality, and I would discover the old ways; I would discover Sophia, goddess of wisdom. My persistent nagging quest had led me in 2002 to the gates of Pacifica Graduate School in Summerland, California, where I became a student of Depth Psychology.

Pacifica and philosophy had called me and grabbed me by the throat. It was a mystical calling that I followed. My heart was blown open by the work. Carl Jung's prolific writings, his psychological, philosophical, spiritual and poetic concepts and processes, and his life story and dreams answered many of my life's questions and quandaries. It was one of the most important adventures of my life. I wrote a philosophical dissertation that focused on Futuristics and included elements of cultural anthropology, social psychology and systems science, titled: Cultural Futuristics: Bringing Consciousness to Cultural Complexes and Soul to Scenario Based Planning.

## Futuristics

Futuristics refers to the futures studies that came into existence in the mid-20th century in an effort to imagine how yesterday and today's realities produced the future. Analyzing patterns and causes of both change and stability from various interdisciplinary perspectives futurists sought to develop maps of alternative futures. They described these alternative futures by writing multiple scenarios that imagined possible, probable, and preferable social, educational, ecological, and political systems. The questions I asked, contemplated and researched in my dissertation were: how is the past creating the present and future? What can we learn from the past in order to avoid global and personal disasters in the future? Do we have a say in all of this? What is our contribution, our responsibility?

I examined films, literature, art, great works of engineering and technological innovations, and came to understand them as prospective in nature. These works were fashioned from ideas that rose to the surface from artists, writers and inventors' imagination and contained the seeds of something not yet known, perhaps a gift from the future. We see these gifts from the future in our daily lives today—everywhere!

Think of Star Trek, the early TV series, for example. The writers invented whole worlds and a starship that traveled where no starship had gone before. The writers populated their stories with imaginative gadgets such as the food replicator, the universal translator, tablet computers, and the tri-corder. The tri-corder was a handheld device that scanned for geological, biological and meteorological anomalies. In 2012, Peter Jansen from McMaster University in Ontario built a working prototype that scanned for magnetic fields and other interference. The food replicator can be seen as the ancestor to today's recycling technology, and the universal translator—translating spoken languages in real-time communication—the parent of simultaneous translation.

Or, take, Sir Arthur C. Clark, the science fiction author most famously known for 2001: A Space Odyssey. Clarke was a lifelong proponent of space travel. In 1934, while still a teenager, he joined the British Interplanetary Society and in 1945, he proposed a satellite communication system. He wrote about these ideas in his books, and as scientists and engineers read them, the geo stationary communication satellites were designed, built, and launched into space. Everything, from GPS to our smartphones to our tablet computers and all other technological inventions, is a direct result of these ideas and stories that had come from thoughts or dreams or insights in someone's mind.

Here is another example: Elon Reeve Musk is a South African-born Canadian-American business magnate, investor, engineer, inventor and founder of SolarCity, Tesla, and SpaceX. His vision is to change the world and humanity. His goals include reducing global warming through sustainable energy production and consumption, and reducing the "risk of human extinction" by "making life multiplanetary" by setting up a human colony on Mars.

He hates leaving his SpaceX headquarters at Hawthorne airport (HHR) in Los Angeles because of the incredible Los Angeles traffic congestion. Thinking like a designer and using the energy of his traffic-inspired-frustration he dreamed up the idea of a super-fast underground tube, train-pod that was inspired by a Sci-fi drawing he had seen in his youth. He called it the Hyperloop, and now, it's been dubbed "the train of the future." It combines magnetic levitation with reduced pressure tubes for a smooth and super fast ride. It can be designed to work above or below ground. Projects are now in planning stages in Dubai, Canada, the Czech Republic and Russia. These are the first steps to connect all of Europe with the Hyperloop, the train of the future.

This is the value of science fiction and the power of the imagination to create a future. Everything in the material world has its inception in thought. That which we can imagine we can create. Way Ahead—is a dream into action project!

## Cultural Futuristics and the Three Future Scenarios

One of the missing perspectives in traditional futures studies, which up to that point preoccupied itself mainly with engineering, logic and technology was the viewpoint of Depth Psychology: calling forth on the wisdom of the heart and soul, and the old traditions and ways that celebrated and relied on symbols, myths and indigenous stories. In speaking about Cultural Futuristics, my dissertation suggests the application of Carl Jung's healing analysis to society and culture—considering society as if it were a client in Jungian therapy. So how would we analyze, for example, such events as those of September the 11th, 2001 in New York, if it were a client facing a Jungian analyst? How could this approach heal the "client" and help shape a better future?

We begin by using the principles of analytical psychology while holding an attitude akin to the Western Apache's theory of wisdom. This means opening up to the highest qualities of the human mind, becoming patient and unhurried in our decisions, and avoiding emotions and actions born of fear, pride, hostility and anxiety. With a calm, poised mind we search for that which is behind the visible surface of reality for the field where morality and imagination meet. We call on stories and myths from diverse cultures to inspire us, we tune into our dreams and synchronicities, and, as the Western Apache would do, we follow our clairvoyant flashes and intuitive insights into action. We call this preliminary stage of Cultural Futuristics our *research*.

Applying such research to 9/11 revealed a number of unconscious motivating forces festering within a world in which such a terrifying and haunting catastrophe occurred. It included fundamentalism, racism, the ruthless dominion of the military industrial complex, and the conflicting opposites between what is known as the "West" and "The Other." The Western Apache wisdom called for probing into the causes of those unconscious forces, taking responsibility for and healing their effects, and reformulating a future devoid of such violent threads.

There have been endless investigations and discussions and assumptions and books written and films made about 9/11—it is the rite of passage of a generation, it changed our world, it has become a collective and personal crossroads—a new myth. No one point-of-view has offered a precise explanation, but one thing 9/11 clearly demonstrated: our world, like the village in a province in China in the story of the Rainmaker, has been out of Tao—out of balance and harmony with the natural laws. So what do we do with this story? This new myth?

Through the method of Cultural Futuristics I have tried to penetrate the pith of this fallen fruit. The deeper story that was excavated from the preliminary research stage I used as intelligence to write three future scenarios.

Similar to the Western Apache method of recounting and drawing inspiration from stories depicting events that happened long ago, Cultural Futuristics focuses on traumatic events and their destructive effects globally and personally. In indigenous cultures and in the Western Apache tradition such events are regarded as a "crossroads"—a hub of many forces that collide with each other to create a breakdown that may very well lead to a breakthrough. These traumatic events are also regarded as "places" and the medicine as "water." Living in harmony with nature, the Native Americans, like the Taoists, understood the parallels between the logic and symmetries of nature and those of human life. It is this understanding that gave rise to such poetic and metaphoric terminology as "place" and "water." Cultural Futuristics adopted similar viewpoints and terminology, aiming to return us to Apache Wisdom, to the Tao, to what psychology calls a "tendency toward consciousness." In other words toward respect for human life, animals, and the natural world.

The three future scenarios—Probable, Preferable and Possible—describe, amongst many things, the integration of the split-off opposites while exposing one-sided demagoguery. They postulate the potentially devastating effects that unconscious-cultural complexities would have in the future if they were not made conscious. If the behavior of a child who plays with guns or tortures cats is not dealt with and the unconscious motives are not detected and healed early on, this child may very well turn into a mass murderer. As in the micro, so in the macro!

I wrote my PhD dissertation in 2004. Following the research stage, I wrote three future scenarios that could have resulted subsequently from the events of September 11, 2001. Here they are in brief, and include the consequences we see now, fifteen years after 9/11, and twelve years after I wrote these scenarios in my dissertation.

## 1. The Probable Scenario

Albert Einstein said, that, "No problem can be solved from the same level of consciousness that created it." Echoing Einstein's postulate, the Probable Scenario describes what will happen when we don't make a change in consciousness, when we act out of pride, fear and retribution, a knee jerk reaction based on the old myth of "an eye-for-an-eye." It describes what will happen when we don't become aware of our shadow—that part of ourselves we are unaware of but are unconsciously driven by. The Probable Scenario is the outcome of not taking responsibility for our blunders and instead acting out of inertia, without asking why, without examining the forces at play, continuing to do what we've done all along and expecting different results—which is one of the definitions for insanity. The Probable Scenario I wrote as the outcome of 9/11 included the following reflections and forecasts:

"Humanity is at one of the most critical points in human history. Resources are fast being depleted, hundreds of millions live in crushing poverty, and changing climatic conditions ravage and alter the face of the earth. Capitalism, globalization, America's addiction to oil and its insatiable consumer appetite have constructed a materialistic monster—an economic machine that can be manipulated to the disadvantage of "We The People" and the entire democratic political system."

"Both the religious fundamentalists in America and in Islamic cultures have fallen into a state of ignorance and intellectual weakness, analogous to pathological obsessive neurosis that takes over rational, clear, intelligent and wise thinking. In the medium run, things fall apart: democracy and human rights are early casualties, nationalism metastasizes, and the disintegration of civilization is the end result. America has already started this downward spiral with domestic surveillance, the Patriot Act, and rejection of the Geneva Conventions."

In retrospect we can see that the US's response to 9/11 was, and still is, the Probable Scenario to the "t." "We'll bomb you back to the Stone Age," was George Bush's knee jerk reaction, his "eye for an eye" call to war, using 9/11 to gain control of Middle East oil supplies under the ploy of bringing democracy to the region.

It is now common knowledge that the war on Iraq was unwarranted, Sadam Hussein did not have weapons of mass destruction, and Iraq was not behind 9/11. The American people had been blatantly lied to in order to justify the war. It is common knowledge that the Iraq war destabilized the region, strengthened Islamic fundamentalism, and gave rise to ISIS and other extremist factions. The worldwide death and destruction inflicted by such groups in the name of Islam—a complete distortion of the faith—has exponentially increased an already ravaging Islamophobia that followed 9/11.

The Probable Scenario played out in the aftermath of 9/11 gave rise to more wars in the Middle East that killed hundreds of thousands, destroyed entire cities, and created multiple refugee crises. It led to global financial catastrophes, ecological destruction, the rise of police violence against blacks, Muslims and other minorities in the US, and to the abuse of human rights and social justice around the world, including Intel infringement on privacy by the National Security Agency (NSA).

While these are only a few of the Probable Scenario consequences of 9/11, and while my scenario clearly foresaw the world becoming increasingly unstable and chaotic—the present global situation has surely surpassed my worst nightmares.

## 2. The Preferable Scenario

This scenario is 180 degrees opposite to the Probably Scenario, and describes what will happen if we take Albert Einstein's advice and solve the problem with a higher consciousness than the one that created it. The Preferable Scenario I wrote as the outcome of 9/11 included the following reflections and forecasts:

"One sided superiority is alleviated with politically diverse voices and a psychological awareness that all societies and cultures are permeated with wisdom. Shadow integration is undertaken by individuals, communities and nation states, and particularly by decision makers in governmental bodies who wisely implement the waging of peace. Greed, avarice and scarcity are replaced with notions of sufficiency and caring. This shift embodies a move from fundamental conceptions of humanity as sinners to notions of wholeness and "paradise within." It calls for people and cultures to work together and spread human rights and social justice around the planet, to anticipate problems, and develop ecological and production orientated sustainability."

"This Preferable Scenario is a benefactor of the arts and crafts, culture and education. Traditional wisdom is highly valued and the contributions of philosophers, musicians, dancers—and all the expressive people connected to the voices of soul—are supported financially and politically worldwide. It's a world with care and hope for the future."

In reaction to the 9/11 attacks, this Preferable Scenario suggested that the US could have just stopped! This would have given an unexpected jolt to the perpetrators and their supporters. The US could have asked itself: Why do they hate us so much? Our leaders could have taken responsibility for being the policeman of the world and for the greedy corporations that steal natural resources from African and Asian countries whose citizens are dying of aids and poverty and war. The US could have taken responsibility for its racism toward blacks, Muslim and other minorities, toward the poor, the LGBTQ community, and toward women. The US could have spoken with the "enemy"—after all, it is with the "enemy" that one makes peace!

In this Preferable Scenario, the US could have been inspired by Ramana Maharishi, who, when asked, "How shall we treat others?" answered, "there are no others." Or by Carl Jung who probed, when are we going to realize that those on the other side of the mountain, who we hate so much, are us? But of course, this scenario, while being preferable, was, and still is, unrealistic, utopic, and could have not come to pass in the state of mind and affairs that permeate the US and the rest of world at the beginning of the 21st century.

## 3. The Possible Scenario

This scenario represents the third and new possibility for humanity, a fusion of the first two scenarios—a bridge between the split-off opposites. Similar in concept to the ancient idea of the Chinese Tao, the middle way is not a gray, watered down compromise but a creative synthesis. As part of this Possible Scenario I wrote the following reflections and forecasts in my dissertation:

"The world begins to draw upon a large population that knows how to reframe events and develop new psychologically astute cultural solutions. More people listen and take a chance on imagining alternative futures, and practically build a new future. At the same time, a number of old authorities are discredited and some of the rich and powerful forgo their control, status and power without the spillage of one drop of blood. Many cultures around the planet clamber their way out of a partial disaster and wake up to their potential."

"It is a world with a new morality. Appreciation for diversity leads to unity in action toward positive growth, peace and racial, economic and environmental justice. Nature is regarded as a delicately complex eco-system in flux, not a mechanism to be engineered and exploited. Ravenous short-term greed is replaced with stewardship of natural resources. Respect for all life creates the right conditions and intentions for sharing in the earth's wealth with all."

"This scenario is an education to reality, a forward step for humanity, and the beginning of a more heartfelt, imaginative and creative engagement with the realities of what has so far been a hostile world. A healthy, inclusive awareness pervades cultures, most importantly in the creation of a new global 'god myth.'"

Fifteen years after 9/11, we see the two polarities described in the Probable and Preferable scenarios standing erect like two sentinels of their own forts. It seems that they will never find the bridge between them. But at the very least, this global reality has now emerged into plain sight. And maybe this awareness is the beginning of true change.

As genocidal wars rage globally over "My God is better than yours," the powers of "light," as they are called, are also blazing! We see "hatred unlimited" between nations, religions, races and genders and between the rich and the poor, but we also see cross-cultural understanding and interfaith communities—where diversity is honored and bridges rather than walls are built—sprouting worldwide.

On the other end of the spectrum of "my God is the true God" there are millions who are not religious but spiritual; they experience God within themselves and in their neighbor and in the in-between. There is emphasis on personal experiential revelations rather than on dogma and scripture. There is an understanding that we are all one. In the US, Europe and other countries we see such reforms as the legalization of same sex marriage, marijuana, and the right to die. We see the protection of human and civil rights for the LGBTQ community. In the US, transgender individuals are permitted to use bathrooms according to their gender identity, even in high schools. Catholic Pope Francis, although not yet authorizing same sex marriage, allows gay couples to receive the sacraments—a radical departure from earlier doctrines.

Attempting to replace the use of oil, we see the emergence of a Green Industry and the creation of new laws to protect the environment. Global climate change is now the most serious threat of all. As the joke (a macabre one) goes: fighting over whose God is better, is like two passengers on the Titanic fighting over a chair.

## From Cultural Futurism to Way Ahead Engineering

My doctoral studies and training experience was exciting intellectually and also helped me understand and heal deep, unresolved family patterns. It alleviated displacement; it lessened my sense of not belonging. The program provided me with an experience wherein I better understood the relationship with my family and in turn with the broader community. The training significantly impacted my inner state. I learned to flow from a state of chaos and confusion to calmer, sober states. This resulted in deeper internal focus and an increasing ability to see myself as determining my own life. I was no longer at the mercy of the circumstances around me. In the haven of Pacifica where I found belonging, I also found freedom and personal independence.

In 2007, as I wore my cap and gown and became a Ph.D. in philosophy, I reflected on a conversation I had had with my mother nearly three decades earlier in which she had shared her fear that I would become a philosopher one day. I also reflected on a dream I had dreamt at age nine, of sitting and writing at the writing desk of philosopher Johann Wolfgang von Goethe in his birth house in Frankfurt am Main in Germany. That dream had been my prophecy revealed to me in the night. My mother's fear had been my rally cry, the red cloak of the bullfighter. Their meeting point was my crossroads!

And so my interest has returned toward personal and individual healing and transformation. Way Ahead is a reworking of my dissertation, and other tools I developed at Pacifica, in service of your individual growth and reorganization of your lives so you can achieve your dreams. It is a method for "Way Forward Engineering" just like Cultural Futuristics, as described in the original dissertation, treated significant cultural events such as 9/11 as dream, as place, and as a client that possesses a veiled, silenced "voice" attempting through action and symptoms to attract humanity's attention.

Way Ahead treats your life—your passion and talents, your traumas and enigmas—as dream, as place, and as your veiled, silenced "voice" attempting through intuition, impulses and synchronicities to attract your attention.

This work will grip you by the throat, and if, as intended, you work the tools beyond just reading the book, you will find the "water" that will heal your soul and nourish your new life. An exciting life! The road you are about to take will pit you face to face with your deepest quest and guide you toward as yet unknown parts of your psyche. The attitude you will be directed to hold will allow for the release of enlightening unconscious material. You will run experiments and access repressed parts of yourself that have been suppressed by circumstances, and you will be guided to dream and record your dreams as they are the royal road to your unconscious, and eventually to the unfolding of your true Self.

2500 years after Oedipus the King, in the more liberal atmosphere of our times, the Mystery Schools of the past meet and fuse at the crossroads with present day scientific and psychological research into the human brain and mind, and with findings in neuroscience and Quantum Physics. This fusion intends to prevent undesirable "prophesied fates" and inspire us to become active participants in the architecture of our own destiny. This is a Way Ahead.

**Way Ahead A Key to Personal Actualizaton**

The Core: Jungian Psychology

Attitude: The Western Apache Mind

Keynote Practice: Journaling

Evaluation: Renee Descartes' Scientific Method

Writing the Three Scenarios: The Probable, The Preferable and The Possible

# THE CORE

# JUNGIAN PHILOSOPHY

## CHAPTER TWO
# Why Way Ahead?

*"When an inner situation is not made conscious,*

*it appears outside as fate."*

*~ Carl G. Jung*

In the age of technological complexity and sophistication, everybody knows that OS is the acronym for Operating System, the basic motor that runs a computer. But what is Way Ahead? It is the science, art and craft of designing your destiny. It is a soulful technology.

## Destiny and Fate

We must begin by understanding what destiny is and what distinguishes it from fate. Fate is the preordained set of realities we are born into, which to a great extent shape our lives. The place, era and time of our birth, the political regime dominating that place at the time, the gender we are born into, the color of our skin, our health, our physical features, our family's economic, religious, ethnic and cultural background, to name a few examples. We have no control over these. There are other factors that inevitably impact our lives and can be referred to as fate such as war, an earthquake, or a tsunami.

Destiny on the other hand is how we navigate within a fated reality, and is the outcome of our personal choices and engagement. There are those who say that destiny is what our life was meant to be, what we were meant to be. Within the set of events in our lives that are preordained, we have free will and can take an active course in shaping our future. There are those born into utter poverty but study and work hard and become extremely successful. There are those who experience childhood trauma in war or by sexual abuse but heal and develop into leaders in our communities; those who are born into a racist society and find ways to claim their human and civil rights and change the course of history, and those born into repressive religions who stand up for their needs. Destiny is what we do to reshape our life and that of our family, community or country despite the realities and events we have been dealt by fate.

Dr. Carl Jung postulated that that which is not made conscious is doomed to manifest as fate. This is THE CENTRAL IDEA OF THIS BOOK, one ingenious idea that sits close to my heart, one that I have been examining, contemplating and striving to live by. I will you give an example:

For his entire life a man traveled the world and took thousands of photographs. It was his hobby, what he loved to do, while at the same time holding a freelance job in the film industry. Whenever he showed his photographs to his friends they all said, "You must make a book, you must have an exhibition." But this man had no desire to show his work beyond his group of friends, he had no ambition for fame or success, and always replied with: "I am not going to do it, but if you want to, go ahead."

In his early sixties, a life threatening illness befell him. He was too weak to work the long and strenuous hours a film industry job required, and he needed money to support his young son. So he decided to design and self publish a book of his photographs and he made an exhibition. It was a unique exhibition, creative and imaginative like no other. Hundreds came. Hundreds of photographs and books were bought. He confided in a friend, "This is what I have wanted to do all my life."

From a Jungian perspective this man's ambition, his ego desire to be in the public eye, and his need for the pleasure that fame and success could bring had all been repressed in his unconscious. This is true, and, this man's photography had a soul of its own and wanted to express itself out in the world, because it knew it could bring healing to the man. He was not conscious of and did not know those parts of himself, thus, they were doomed to somehow, someday, manifest as fate. In his case it took a life threatening illness to force him to unlock his unconscious and allow the soul of the work to express itself and sing the song of his healing heart. He is happy, transformed, the life threatening illness is no longer a threat, and a photo exhibition that is a real life story in pictures has been shared with hundreds.

## The Oracle

Two and a half millennia before Carl Jung, way before the emergence
of psychology as a scientific discipline in the 19th century and before
such terms as "conscious" and "unconscious" had become household
names, we find carved into the entrance to the ancient temple of
Delphi in Greece the phrase "Know Thyself." The temple of Delphi
was the abode of the Oracle, the entity that could see the future
and was consulted on important decisions in the ancient classical
world, from political decisions to those of a personal nature. The
idea that knowing oneself and knowing one's future were interlaced,
has been recognized since the beginning of human civilization and
has held a fascination for all people.

*Figure 3: L0011572: Wellcome Library, London Reconstructions of the sacred
precints at Epidaurus*

From a Native American prophecy that foretells the birth of the "Rainbow Warriors" who will save the earth from environmental destruction, to the biblical prophecy about a time in our far away future in which "the wolf will dwell with the lamb and the calf with the lion," to tea leaf and coffee readers, psychic readers, the tarot, astrology, the iChing, the ruins, palmistry, numerology, and the many other forms of divination we can see the importance the future holds on us politically, spiritually, financially, and in matters of the heart.

Why this fascination? Because we want to know how things will turn out, we are impatient, we can't just sit still in the present moment, we desire love and money and success, and we want to know now that we will get it, so we can rest assured. But more importantly, this fascination comes from a deep knowing inside that our destinies are not just fated and that by knowing, for example, "the position of the stars in the sky" we can modify and change the trajectory of our lives. Think about the weather forecast. It is fated that it is going to rain. You can disregard it and walk out in a t-shirt and without an umbrella and get sick, or you can take an umbrella with you and go out singing in the rain.

We often feel that we are destined to attain a certain goal or desire, like selling a product, having more clients, or meeting the love of our life, but something happens and our "destined future" does not come to pass. We think it's an accident. But is it? There is no absolute answer to this question. There are areas in personal and societal life in which we have control over events and can even foresee their outcome, yet there is a vast range of situations, conditions and events that are out of our control.

Way Ahead is not a divination tool for knowing the future, but a modality that inspires vision, design and implementation of our most valuable goals.

In the realm of future predictions there is the trap of falling into the pit hole of superstition, even dogma. As goes the story of the horse with the white foot. A man and his young son bought a horse that had one white foot. The horse had a wonderful disposition, was strong and beautiful and won many horse races and competitions. Later, they bought a horse that had four white feet and was shortly killed. After the father died, the son, who was now the business owner, came up with the solution for future success in buying a horse. It stated, "If it has one white foot buy him, two white feet try him, three white feet look well about him, four white feet do well without him."

Or the story of the Zen monastery and the cat. A Zen master and his students were sitting in deep meditation when a cat outside the monastery hall began to meow. Afterwards the students commented on how deep their meditation had been. When the Zen master got ill and left this world, one of the students became the new master and implemented a new rule for his students. It stated: "When we meditate, make sure we always have a cat meowing outside the monastery hall."

Way Ahead is not a superstition or dogma, nor is it a set of mathematical equations that will bring about an exact knowable outcome in your life. It is rather a technology of the soul that combines the philosophy and wisdom and practices of the old ways with the knowledge of the most advanced scientific discoveries of our times. It is a creative and imaginative path that invites you to know thyself, to understand your past and align yourself with the winds of the present. To examine and understand the twists and turns in your life, what caused them, what could have been avoided, were you erred and where you were successful. To recognize your unique talents and gifts, your virtues and flaws, your flashes of inspiration and insight and vision, and your persistent intuitions. This multilayered journey will harness and engage your whole self in service of designing three future scenarios for your life – probable, possible and preferable – then choosing and implementing one of the scenarios.

## The OS of a Computer and Way Ahead

The operating system is the most important program that runs on a computer. It knows and performs basic tasks such as recognizing input from the keyboard, sending output to the desktop, keeping track of files, and controlling peripheral devices such as drives and printers. It is like a traffic cop: it makes sure that different programs and users running at the same time do not interfere with each other, and it is responsible for security and for ensuring that unauthorized users do not access the system. For a computer's operating system to function at its highest performance it requires maintenance.

We can think of the basic functions that make a human being "tick" as our existing basic operating system: it directs the heart to beat, the lungs to breathe, the brain to think, and the blood to flow in our veins. It is responsible for such natural instincts and reflexes as fight or flight, blushing, being tickled, and such physiological urges as hunger or the process of procreation or digestion. All of these are autonomic functions—we have no control over them (unless we are a fakir in India)—they are inherent to being a living, breathing human being or animal.

In the world of computers we run applications such as spreadsheets, writing programs like Word or Final Draft and art programs like Photoshop on top of the basic operating system. In the world of humans, Way Ahead is an upgrade—an enhancement—of our existing operating system—and on top of that we run "applications" to help us design a house, write a screenplay, advocate for world peace, or become the best spouse and parent. If we want to achieve our dreams and goals in life we better be engaged in designing them, lest we risk swaying like a boat lost at sea or a feather in the wind. Imagine! In designing your destiny, you do not run yourself to the ground, you do not crash your bank account or rob a bank. Instead, you create visionary projects that support your overall wellbeing, physically, emotionally, spiritually, financially and ethically.

## Contemplation

What might be repressed within you?

1.................................................................................................................

...........................................................................................................

...........................................................................................................

..................................................................................................

..................................................................................................

..................................................................................................

2...............................................................................................

..................................................................................................

..................................................................................................

..................................................................................................

3...............................................................................................

..................................................................................................

..................................................................................................

..................................................................................................

What would pop up if the door to your unconscious would be unlocked?

1...............................................................................................

..................................................................................................

..................................................................................................

..........................................................................................

2...........................................................................................

..........................................................................................

..........................................................................................

..........................................................................................

3...........................................................................................

..........................................................................................

..........................................................................................

..........................................................................................

Who would pop in through the door of your unconscious and what would they say to you?

1...........................................................................................

..........................................................................................

..........................................................................................

..........................................................................................

2. .........................................................................................................

.........................................................................................................

.........................................................................................................

.........................................................................................................

3. .........................................................................................................

.........................................................................................................

.........................................................................................................

.........................................................................................................

.........................................................................................................

.........................................................................................................

.........................................................................................................

.........................................................................................................

.........................................................................................................

## CHAPTER THREE
# CARL JUNG PART 1
## Depth Psychology, the Shadow & the Battle of Opposites

*"The psychological rule says that when an inner situation is not made*

*conscious, it happens outside, as fate. That is to say, when the*

*individual remains undivided and does not become conscious*

*of his inner opposite, the world must perforce act out the*

*conflict and be torn into opposing halves."*

*~ Carl G. Jung*

As stated earlier, this profound and revolutionary statement by Carl Jung is the essence of Way Ahead. In this chapter we'll examine a few fundamental Jungian concepts such Individuation, the Shadow, and the Opposites—all of which are components of the broad field of Depth Psychology, components you will explore and take into consideration when designing your Way Ahead.

## Depth Psychology

Depth Psychology is an interdisciplinary endeavor that draws on literature, philosophy, poetry, mythology, the arts, as well as science and logic. The term was coined at the turn of the 20th century by Eugen Bleuler, a professor of psychiatry at the University of Zürich and director of the Burghölzli Asylum in Zürich, where Carl Jung began his career as a psychiatrist.

Depth Psychology views the human being as often divided against itself, with some thoughts, feelings, wishes and memories accessible to awareness, and others that have been exiled from it and are hidden beneath the surface. By focusing on the unconscious, Sigmund Freud, Carl Jung and their followers worked to chart and delineate a path that makes the unconscious, conscious. Through the study of dreams, images, symptoms, slips of the tongue, spontaneous humor, meaningful coincidences and connections to humans and all things, depth psychologists attempt to understand the language of the unconscious.

Depth Psychology's approach to psychological suffering focuses on helping individuals and communities become aware of what has been cast out of consciousness and not yet able to be known.

In Jung's theory, postulating that "...when the individual remains undivided and does not become conscious of his inner opposite, the world must perforce act out the conflict and be torn into opposing halves," the word "undivided" refers to the conscious and unconscious that have not yet split and the person is still unaware of the different parts of oneself. But growth and wisdom only begin with the awareness of one's many parts, when the unconscious is made conscious. Healing is the fruit of allowing that which has been repressed, rejected, denied or ignored to come forward so that a person or a community can understand and explore the significance of the revealed material, integrate it, and open up to a transformation in consciousness.

My own journey has led me to understand the role of symbolic experiences, dreams, significant events, seemingly chance encounters and coincidences as harbingers of my future. Our biographies are of great significance in understanding our current circumstances, and our current circumstances contain the seeds for future growth and development. Incorporating Depth Psychology practices into designing your future is essential in turning your wishes and visions into a new reality, and your dreams of the night into the actions of the day.

## Individuation

The goal of Jungian analysis and essentially of Way Ahead is what Jung called Individuation: the achievement of a greater degree of consciousness in our psychological, interpersonal and cultural experiences. It is the process of becoming our unique, individual selves—free of the destructive and inauthentic patterns of belief and behavior we have been programmed to be by family, society and the culture at large. It is the process of becoming whole, becoming who we were meant to be, destined to be. We cannot become whole without first recognizing the divisions within us. We cannot become individuated until we separate our parts and then put them back together again. Like when buying a product at IKEA that comes in parts and then we put them together to become a chair or a table. This so-called "Individuation" is both a healing process and a goal. The process leads us to discover our specific life purpose—and live the kind of life we excitedly wake up to every morning. In the broadest possible way, individuation can be seen and experienced as the achievement of self-actualization through a process of integrating the conscious and the unconscious.

## The Shadow & the Battle of Opposites

The Oracle of Delphi, the beautiful human mistress of the god Apollo, had the power to enter into ecstatic communion with him and deliver prophesies to the world. She was known as Pythia, derived from the word pythein that refers to the sickly, sweet smell of the decomposing body of the Python snake after it had been slain by Apollo.

The Temple at Delphi, house of Pythia, where inscribed at the entrance was the directive Know Thyself, was also known as the House of Snakes. From time immemorial the snake has represented the epitome of fright and disgust for young and old all over the world. In contrast, it has been revered by indigenous people as a symbol for spiritual transformation, and by western medicine as a symbol for healing—a symbol you find on every medical building sign in the form of two intertwining snakes on a staff. The opposites. A curse, a monstrous creature, is also a therapeutic and transformative power. "He is a snake" is an expression for someone cruel and frightening. In the biblical story in Genesis, the snake had walked on two legs before it ate from the forbidden fruit and was expelled from Eden and cursed to crawl on its belly forever. In Jungian studies the snake is recognized as a universal archetypal image, and often comes in dreams to those who first enter therapy or begin a practice of meditation. The appearance of the snake in a dream signifies psychological progress or spiritual initiation.

There is a "snake" in each one of us. It lives in what Carl Jung called The Shadow, which is housed in our unconscious. The Shadow is comprised of all the aspects in our personality that we deny and hide, that we do now "own." It was created in childhood, our formative years. Anything that did not fit the status quo of family beliefs, traditions, religion, the new age, the party-line—you name it—anything that was too unique or too unconventional was deemed unacceptable and undesirable and suppressed into the Shadow, into the darkness of the unconscious—hidden and unknown even to ourselves. "Knowing thyself," means getting to know all those parts of ourselves: the conscious and its opposite, the unconscious. This is the cornerstone of designing our OS.

*Figure 4: Shadow play on sunny Australian Beach by Mario Hoppmann*

We must know what we love, what we are good at, as well as the parts of ourselves that caused us to behave in ways we do not understand. These aspects of our personality that have been repressed into the Shadow manifest as negative tendencies and behaviors such as depression, rage, apathy, violence or addiction. We perceive this Shadow as negative. But it is not! The Shadow is the seat of our creativity and all of our wonderful unique qualities, talents and abilities. But because these had been suppressed and disrespected by our upbringing or culture they retreated, or been forced, into the Shadow and there they turned into their opposite. Unusual leadership ability may have turned into obsessive control; a talent for dance into introversion; natural healing in an illness. In racist societies, we find those who are discriminated against begin to modify their behavior in order to fit in. But at a high price: their shame, humiliation and guilt are repressed into the unconscious and may very well show up one day as violence toward oneself or others.

Paradoxically, while we don't see our own Shadow and the flaws and virtues in it, we see those same flaws and virtues in the other and we resent or admire them, respectively. This is the phenomenon known as projection, negative or positive: we loathe the thief; we fall head over heels with the movie star. But what do we project onto the thief that we are blindsided to in ourselves? And what is our own movie star quality that we don't recognize?

Designing our destiny requires a bit of soul excavation. We must discover and understand the operating system that was installed in us in childhood and has unconsciously been controlling our lives to this day. By making the unconscious conscious we will prevent it from crashing our souls and destroying our bodies without us even knowing why. How many times have you asked yourself "Why can't I meet a life partner?" or "Why can't I make more money?" Much of the answers could be found in the unconscious. In nature, a shadow is the space where light from a light source is blocked by an opaque object. A shadow created by a strong source of light will be darker than the one created by a lesser light source. So in life, the brighter the light, the darker the shadow. That's why influential figures recognized and approved by society are likely to have a more "shadowy" side to their personality: brilliant and successful actors and politicians are often insecure or fearful or prone to alcoholism; religious officials are discovered to have sexually abused children or women caught under their "holy" spell; or homophobes who are themselves closeted homosexuals. This is the Battle of Opposites.

**To design our destiny, it is imperative that we recognize and own our projections and balance the destructive opposites within us. Then and only then will the opposites alchemically blend together, like two sensual Latin dancers or a superb jazz ensemble.**

## Integrating the Opposites

There are pairs of opposites within each one of us: the introvert versus the extrovert, the sensualist versus the ascetic, the emotional versus the thinker, the confident versus the timid, the poet versus the philosopher, the rational versus the intuitive, the rebel versus the compliant, the millionaire versus the cockroach, and so on. We experience the split between the opposites in us as extreme torment, often as being "crucified between" them, or as being taken over by one or the other, driving our lives into a collision or over a cliff without any control on our part in the matter.

The core of the Jungian project is the reconciliation of the opposites. It requires first becoming aware of them. "By bearing the opposites," wrote Jung, "we can expose ourselves to life in our humanity ... we have to risk life to get into life, then it takes on color." Often this is terribly difficult and painful. This turn you are taking at the crossroads does have consequences. So be mindful. It is known as the "road less travelled" and as the "warrior's path." It requires courage, vigilance and faith.

In order to upgrade our basic operating system to Way Ahead we must discover our opposites. We do this by examining our lives inside out with rigor and sincerity: our past from childhood onward, the messages we get from our dreams in the night, the feedback we receive from friends and family and associates, and from life itself. We pay attention to the feelings that specific situations evoke in us. All these are stations along the way to acceptance of ourselves as we are, and acceptance is the first step towards change.

Accepting and holding the tension between the opposites, allowing ourselves to feel the forceful pull of the two directions, eventually reveals the "reconciling third,"—a transcendental euphoric moment that Jung called the experience of the Self.

Let's take the example of a woman split between rebellion and compliance. For most of her life she pretty much marched to her own tune, breaking norms, until she found herself in a financial crisis. She now had to do a job that required of her to work on the weekend. On this particular Sunday all she wanted to do was just lie on her bed and watch a TV series. That was her rebellious part, directing her to do what she wanted, when she wanted it. But she had a deadline on her writing project. She stood there crucified between these two needs—and she allowed herself to feel the allure of both. And then the "reconciling third" arose. She patiently cooked for herself a soup to eat later, and remembering how much she loved her writing project she sat down and worked with great pleasure. After finishing a first draft she lay on her bed and watched an episode of the TV series she liked, before returning to her desk. Maybe what's most important is the exhilaration that possessed her as she did all this: cooking the soup, the writing, and watching the TV episode.

Jung described the process that leads to the "reconciling third" as an alchemical melting together of the opposites. As in alchemy where base materials are turned into gold, so in human life, the coming together of opposites releases the vital creative energy that was stuck in the tension between them. This release may be experienced as peacefulness, or as a whirlwind or a tornado.

The mask we wear in the world, the part of us we know and are proud of, is our clue to its opposite found in the depth of our Shadow. Just look 180 degrees in the opposite direction and you'll find it. Hold them and discover the reconciling—alchemical—transcendent—third. The process of designing our destiny leads us to that state of being, and also asks of us to be in that state in order to design it. It's a marriage between our wounds and our creativity, our Light and our Shadow. Expansion of consciousness and increased ability to live between the two levels of reality, material and spiritual, external and internal are the hard won prize.

# CHAPTER FOUR

# UTOPIA & ARMAGEDDON: A PERSONAL STORY

*"Just as high always longs for low and hot for cold, so all consciousness,*

*perhaps without being aware of it, seeks its unconscious opposite...*

*Life is born only of the spark of opposites."*

*~ Carl G. Jung*

From a young age my life has dealt me a deck of cards full of so-called opposites, and I have always walked the path of seeking to understand and harmonize them for the sake of my wellbeing and that of the world.

During my childhood in New Zealand no one ever spoke about the Great Wars, the Füehrer, or anti-Semitism. Genocide was never mentioned nor was Vladimir Lenin's death squad that assassinated my Russian grandfather in 1918. For the first seven years of my life I lived in my Russian grandmother's house—Casa Bobo, as I used to call it—three blocks from the beach, in Lyall Bay, a small seaside suburb of Wellington. My Oma Bobo ran a boarding house in our two-story Victorian weatherboard charmer. She was warm and loving and cooked delicious Russian meals, especially red Borst, with Kasha and a dollop of sour cream on top.

Lyall Bay, Wellington's surf beach, was the location for the annual surf lifesaving championships and had earlier been known as "False Bay," after the captain of the ship Winwick had misread the bay for the actual entrance to the Wellington harbor. The Maori, the indigenous people of New Zealand, had named the beach Huetepara—"The Ripe Gourd"—and Ripe Gourd was my home, my Utopia.

As the insecure child of immigrants who had left their German and Russian civilizations behind when they immigrated to New Zealand, I was estranged and alienated from any culture—German, Russian, or Kiwi. As is the case with Utopia, it has no concrete location in time or place...

**My Utopia had no past, no kin, no community,**

**nor any local history that could tie me**

**to the place.**

All I ever read was science fiction, all I ever thought about was the future. Fantasizing about an ever-mythical future assuaged a deep longing in me and provided an aureole of hope around tomorrow's adventures.

*Figure 5: Distant view of Port Nicholson, Wellington, 1857, by Vincent Brooks.*

Later we moved to a house that sat perched atop a range of hills overlooking the entrance to Wellington's harbor. Situated on a major fault line, the land around the harbor had been torn open by a major earthquake that had created unusual geological formations around the turquoise water of the bay. The entrance to the harbor could be quite dangerous, its strait notoriously rough, its rocks breaking the water's surface at low tide. For a sensitive boy like myself, the harbor, its Maori name Tara, and the stories that accompanied it were pure magic. It was here that the inter-island passenger ferry Wahine grounded during a storm with the loss of fifty-one lives. I went to school that day, walking down to the bus stop in a howling gale only to arrive at the school hours later and find out that the storm had turned into a hurricane and the school had been closed. I went to a friend's house, all the phone lines were down and no one knew where I was. My older Sister Renata went looking for me and watched the Wahine ground itself on the reef.

The capsizing of the Wahine and the grave loss of life threw a wrench into my innocent and idealized view of the world—my Utopia. But I continued to watch the inter-island ferries shuttling passengers back and forth between the north and south islands every day and once took a trip on it myself. On my way down I painted a picture of a sailing ship and drew crowds while I was painting it. Since then I have been greatly influenced by places of arrival and departure, seaports, airports, metro stations. Way Ahead in a sense is a book about this crossroads, about a moment in time where you both depart and arrive...

When I was nine years old, my mother became a Jehovah's Witness. She became a fanatic and I became doomed to live under the fear of "Armageddon's imminent arrival." Every morning, the moment my mother would hear my father's Volkswagen engine burst into life, she would point her finger and direct me to sit at the kitchen table, she would pull out her bible, and we would continue studying the lesson from the day before. Interspersed with these studies she would enroll me into believing that our eventual salvation was impending.

> "Salvation is a gift from God," she would teach me, "attained by being part of 'God's Organization' and putting our faith in Jesus's sacrifice." She would quiz me as to the two types of resurrection.

> "We believe in different forms of resurrection," I would answer her, "one group, the anointed ones, like us, are part of the 144,000 who will go to the everlasting Heaven and

rule beside God, while "the other sheep" or "the great crowd" will live forever on earth in Paradise."

"Excellent!" she would exclaim.

Often at this point she would say that Paradise wouldn't be so bad because it would be summer all year round and it would never rain, nor would there be earthquakes or unhappiness or destituteness. I would always think that I wanted it to rain, I wanted to feel poor or lonely, I wanted the earthquakes to happen—how else could magical places come about? The last words my mother would say to me every morning at the end of our lesson was, "You and I will be two of the 144,000."

I needed to find a way to live between hope and fear. I instinctively understood that the idea of Armageddon and the inevitable apocalypse merely hid the insecurity and chaos that a terrifying and unknown future held. Yet the magical place of my childhood—where many years later The Lord of the Rings movie series would be filmed and where much of J. R. R. Tolkien's most widely read works The Hobbit and The Lord of the Rings are set—has been known as "Middle-Earth," short-hand for "Fictional-Universe." In the chasm between Utopia and Armageddon my spirit has escaped. It is also where spirit has entered me.

It is precisely this "Middle Earth," that had once been unknown, that Carl G. Jung discovered for us all. A "Middle Earth," a third place between Armageddon and Utopia. A place between hope and despair, between night and day. This new and alternative place within us is filled with stories and wise guidance. It is what Sigmund Freud called "a royal road to the unconscious." When we discover this place for ourselves we understand that our lives are informed and influenced by the vast Collective Unconscious, by Universal Archetypes, and the synchronistic events that are happening all around us.

CHAPTER 5

# CARL JUNG PART 2

## THE COLLECTIVE UNCONSCIOUS, ARCHETYPES, DREAMS & SYNCHRONICITIES

*"The underlying, primary psychic reality is so inconceivably complex*

*that it can be grasped only at the farthest reach of intuition, and*

*then but very dimly. That is why it needs symbols."*

~ *Carl Jung*

In this chapter we'll examine additional fundamental Jungian concepts such the Collective Unconscious, Universal Archetypes, myths, dreams and Active Imagination—all of which also compose the broad field of depth psychology, components you will be using when designing your Way Ahead.

## The Collective Unconscious & the Archetypes

Sigmund Freud and Carl Jung recognized that one's unresolved traumas and disturbances in early life such as the loss of a parent, sexual or emotional abuse, the pain of exile or war or famine are all stored in the personal unconscious and shape a person's life. Carl Jung's particular insight, however, was his recognition that individuals are also influenced by unconscious factors that lie outside their personal experience and have a universal quality.

Carl Jung wrote: "It must be pointed out that just as the human body shows a common anatomy over and above all racial differences, so, too, the psyche possesses a common substratum transcending all differences in culture and consciousness. I have called this substratum the "Collective Unconscious." It described the part of the unconscious mind, which Jung believed was separate from the personal unconscious and was shared by all members of a particular species. We can imagine the Collective Unconscious as a web of universal interconnectedness.

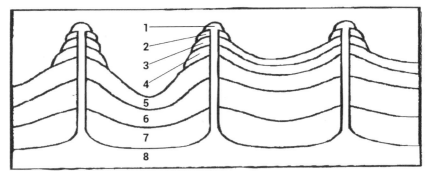

*Figure 6: Reproduction by M. Glock of the original diagram used by Jung to explain the Collective Unconscious. 1:Individual 2: Family 3: Clan 4: Nation 5: Large Group 6: Prieval Ancestors 7: Animal Ancestors 8: Central Fire (The Collective Unconscios)*

In the physical world we can say that humans, animals and all things on the planet share the air, earth and sky. An environmental disaster in one place has the capacity to affect another place far away. Or, as the story goes, the fluttering of the butterfly's wing in Norway can generate a snowstorm in Colorado. So in the spiritual world, the Collective Unconscious is the cauldron from which we all draw and to which we give back. And because we are all connected within this cauldron, one person's healing on one side of the planet might have an implication for another person on the other side. Yes—this is the idea! Our personal dreams and thoughts and deeds, our visions and nightmares, our good and bad intentions all travel in and out of this cauldron, creating an affect on the holographic whole. This is why it's so important to watch our thoughts and our deeds.

**The Collective Unconscious can be understood and experienced as God or Spirit or any other name you give to the primordial, eternal and omnipresent Divine.**

Jung suggested that the Collective Unconscious was made up of archetypes and myths, which are universal symbols, stories and motifs shared by humanity. Archetypes are inborn structures that lie deep within the Collective Unconscious, transcending one's personal biographical experiences and memories, and extending into the wider realm of culture, history, nature, ancestry and spirit. They address how humanity has responded spiritually, philosophically, socially and aesthetically to the grand themes of existence, such as life, death, rebirth, childhood, conflict, relationships, and so on.

Archetypes are universal—viscerally known and belonging to all. Jung believed it was the reason why human beings from all over the world and throughout history had similar myths and thoughts, created similar religions, and used similar symbols even without any direct connection between them. Here are a few examples of basic archetypes that Jung devised:

*The Self:* unification of the individual ego with the personal and Collective Unconsciousness. *The Shadow:* source of the sexual and creative and life instincts.

*Anima and Animus:* the male energies present within the female, and female energies present within the male. *The Father:* authority figure, stern, powerful. *The Mother:* nurturing, comforting. *The Child:* longing for innocence, rebirth, salvation, protection. *The Sage:* guidance, knowledge, wisdom. *The Hero:* champion, defender, rescuer. *The Maiden:* innocence, desire, purity. *The Trickster:* deceiver, troublemaker, liar.

In mythologies from around the world we find a large scope of archetypal models that have inspired humanity for millennia. The Greek goddess Aphrodite for example, is the archetype for love and beauty. The Mona Lisa by Leonardo Da Vinci or the Hollywood actress Marilyn Monroe personifies this archetype. The Aphrodite archetype is also found in the love of an artist for his painting (yes, the Aphrodite energy exists in men too), in a writer for his book, an editor for the film she is editing. The archetype governs the fashion, film and music industries. Aphrodite has been known by different names in different cultures: in the classical Roman period she was Venus, in Indian culture she is Lalita, in the bible she is Eve. These were not/are not real human beings, but mythic, symbolic descriptions of aspects and qualities that exist in all humans.

It is said that a myth is something that has never happened but happens all the time. Each one of us is comprised of various mythic and universal archetypes. This is why a woman from a rural village in Africa will meet a woman from New York City and when speaking about a Wise Old Man they will understand each other, even if the New Yorker Wise Old Man wears a three-piece suit and tie, and the African Wise Old Man wears a lungi.

Carl Jung wrote, "An archetype is an original model of a person, an ideal example, or a prototype upon which others are copied, patterned or emulated; a symbol universally recognized by all ... a model of a person, personality, or behaviour."

Endless myths from around the world give voice to the universal human dilemmas and paradoxes, probing into the un-answerable questions about life and death, creation and destruction, good and evil, destiny and free will. Here are a few examples:

## Creation Myth· Mother Earth and Father Sky

"How was the world created?" is a question both physics and religion have addressed whether with measured scientific proof or with story and myth. Mother and father figures usually appear in creation myths: the mother is usually the earth and the father the sky. This may be attributed to the fact that life emerges both from Mother Earth and from the womb of a mother. People of ancient times were mystified by the creation of children and vegetation and found links between mothers and Mother Earth. In calling the sky Father, a sense of unity was created, as in the bonds of matrimony.

In the Greek Creation Myth, the goddess Gaia and the god Uranus fell in love. Uranus was the sky and Gaia the earth. Together they had many children and grandchildren who created the plants, animals, stars and oceans. The unity of Gaia and Uranus created a sense that the universe was one.

In the worldview of the Australian Aborigines, the Sun Mother created all the animals, plants and bodies of water on earth upon the urging of the Father of All Spirits. These two divine beings did not actually have children; only their names reflected the mother-father theme. However, the Sun Mother was portrayed as one that gives life to the sleeping spirits. A human mother also gives life to a spirit.

A Navajo myth speaks about an immortal who created the earth and the sky, and keeps them apart by propping sky on four giants placed at the four compass points. The panting of the giants as they bear the weight of the sky causes the winds and storms.

The first line in Genesis in the bible says: "In the beginning God created the heavens and the earth." Our own planet earth is called Mother Earth. Eastern philosophies speak about the goddess as Divine Mother. Lalita, Laxmi, Tara, Kali, Quan Yin, Shakti are all diverse archetypal expressions of the Mother—out of whom we have all emerged. They are archetypal energies/aspects/tendencies we all possess.

## Flood Myths

In these myths a great flood was usually sent by a deity to destroy civilization, often in an act of divine retribution. Flood stories are common across a wide range of cultures extending back into prehistory, and are also found in certain Creation Myths since the floodwaters are cleansing in preparation for spiritual rebirth. Most Flood Myths contain a hero, who represents the human craving for survival. We find this in the biblical story of Noah's Ark, the large vessel that was built to prevent the destruction of the human race and animal species during the apocalyptic deluge.

The Toltec natives in Mexico have a legend telling that the original creation lasted for 1716 years, and was destroyed by a flood and only one family survived.

A myth from Southwest Tanzania in Africa tells us: once upon a time the rivers began to flood. The God told two people to get into a ship. He told them to take lots of seeds and lots of animals. The water of the flood eventually covered the mountains. Finally the flood stopped. Wanting to know if the water had dried up, one of the people let a dove loose. The dove returned without anything in its beak. It was not time yet to return to the land. Later, a hawk was let loose and did not return. The people understood that the hawk had spied food on the drained landscape, and this allowed them to leave the boat and take the animals and the seeds with them to start a new life.

Flood Myths are archetypal metaphors and allegories for death or destruction that leads to eventual rebirth and renewal. It is a dramatic, emotional and cathartic journey. Water represents fluidity and transformation as it can go from ice to water to steam. It is the ebb and flow of life itself. The water element occupies 70% of our bodies, and prior to our birth the embryonic fluid was our safe home. Water in all its forms—rain, rivers, the sea, the ocean, a storm, snow or steam—is archetypal.

## Mountain Myths

From the beginning of recorded history, the mountain has played a prominent role in mythology and religion. Many religions started on mountains, or their prophets and leaders communed with the Divine on a mountaintop and brought their knowledge down to the people. Jesus of Nazareth kept a 40-day vigil on the mountain to transcend his ego. Moses brought down the tables of the covenant after 40 days of solitude at the top of Mount Sinai. The creator of Reiki energy healing spent 40 days on a mountaintop in Japan and brought down the symbols for Reiki healing. On the top of a mountain, close to the heavens, these men absorbed themselves in self-inquiry, contemplation and meditation, and prepared themselves to advance the evolution of humankind upon their return.

Mountains have also been considered gods, or the homes of the gods. Mount Kailas in the Himalayas in Northern India is believed to be the abode of Shiva, the most important God in Hinduism. It is a sacred mountain, one that every devout Hindu yearns to make a pilgrimage to at least once in a lifetime, to absolve one's sins. Mount Olympus is the highest mountain peak in Greece and was once regarded as the "home of the Greek Gods/The Twelve Olympians of the Hellenistic World."

Mountains appear in contemporary dreams and visions. Climbing a mountain can be seen as a symbol for moving toward a goal or an aspiration, or for rising in one's consciousness or artistic or social evolution.

The Jungian analytical process is intended to bring the symbols and archetypes, both personal and collective, into consciousness, allowing the individual to see more clearly what forces are at play in his or her life. Implicit in Jung's understanding of the archetypes is the creation or uncovering of a goal toward which your life may be directed. The Collective Unconscious and the archetypes and myths are an ocean of inspiration! They speak directly to your soul and will bring about renewed energies when designing your Way Ahead. Your soul is already working toward your future. Follow it.

## Synchronicities, Dreams & Active Imagination

The cliché tells us that synchronicity is God's way of remaining anonymous. Say you're driving in your car early in the morning and you're thinking about the new business you're about to begin, or the interview you'll be having in a couple of hours, or a book you're just starting and just at that moment the sun is coming out, and then, as if out of the blue, the song Here Comes the Sun by the Beatles, comes on the radio. You go, WOW! You feel, ah, what a great omen, God, is telling me something. Right. God is telling you, "Good luck... you're on the right path!" There is no rational explanation why these three events—your thinking of your new beginning, the sunrise, and the Beatles song—all coincide. This is synchronicity. An a-causal connection between two or more events, meaning, one event did not cause the other, each one happened separately and autonomically. Carl Jung coined the term for this connection: synchronicity.

Jung theorized that all beings, animals, animate and non-animate objects, are connected through the Collective Unconscious. Nowadays we call it Oneness.

Jung was influenced by eastern philosophies and their discoveries of five millennia ago about the power of the mind to influence reality, and about the connectedness of all things. He studied the Tao, the writing of Lao Tzu, who wrote: "There is a thing, formless yet complete. Before heaven and earth, it existed. Without sound, without substance, it stands alone and unchanging. It is all pervading and unfailing. We do not know its name, but we call it Tao... being one with nature, the sage is in accord with the Tao."

Similarly, Jung claimed that the psyche interacts with events in the outside world, just like quantum physics has shown that the researcher influences his or her study. Whether we are looking for a logical explanation to a synchronicity, or just call it a coincidence, taking it into consideration, assigning it meaning, can be life changing—a turning point at the crossroads of your destiny. When the person who saw the beautiful sunrise as he was listening to Here Comes the Sun now goes on the job interview or starts his new business or writes the first sentence of his/her book, this person's state of mind will be calmer, more secure, more present, thus allowing for a more effective and inspired performance.

## Synchronicity suggests that the outer world is a reflection of one's inner world.

Carl Jung's concept of synchronicity was prompted by the case of one of his clients. This woman was run by her rationalism and could not open up to her emotional, intuitive side. One night she dreamt of a golden scarab. During the next day's session with Jung, a large insect hit against the stained glass window. When Jung caught it, it was a golden scarab. From his studies of the culture of ancient Egypt, Jung knew that the scarab symbolized death and rebirth. This synchronicity affirmed for Jung the client's necessity for psychological death and rebirth. It was her crossroads, a map for her psychological evolution toward a more balanced relationship between her ego and her unconscious, personal and collective. All that, the scarab came to tell her!

**Synchronicity is not static or theoretical. It is an engine for action, for deeds and for transformation, and so are our dreams, if we are willing to listen and live by them.**

Jung wrote: "Dreams are purposeful. They have the goal of synthesizing experience into images in meaningful and creative methods." Each dream aims toward an expansion of awareness. It teaches, corrects, prophesies and comments; it is the Collective Unconscious breaking through from the depths. Both dreams and outer events can be seen as symbolic messages from a source that sustains and directs the individuation process throughout our dream life. Dreams can be compensatory and complementary; they may challenge an existing view or add a perspective that is unrelated to the conscious position. These are, as Jung postulated, "prospective dreams, ones which anticipate in the unconscious, future conscious achievements, and, thus, for example, provide solutions to conflict in allegoric or symbolic form."

The path between dreams, synchronicity and life itself is what Jung named "Active Imagination." It is the practice of reflection and contemplation on dreams and synchronicities—as he himself did when reflecting on the ancient Egyptology symbol of the scarab. Active Imagination is key to better understanding the dream and its guidance and teaching for the dreamer's life. It bridges between one's conscious and unconscious.

There are many ways to enter Active Imagination: we can meditate and allow our mind to free associate on the dream images, we can imagine the continuation and outcome of the dream, and we can enter deeper into the feelings and emotions the dream has transported us into. Jung was insistent that some form of participation in Active Imagination was essential. He wrote: "You yourself must enter into the process with your personal reactions...as if the drama being enacted before your eyes were real." Of the origin of Active Imagination, he wrote: "I was sitting at my desk once more, thinking over my fears. Then I let myself drop. Suddenly it was as though the ground literally gave way beneath my feet, and I was plunged into the dark depths."

Active Imagination for the purpose of integration and healing can be also done by writing, dancing, making music ... in fact one can say that creativity is an act of Active Imagination, period! Any teacher or facilitator in any art or creative endeavor will tell you that. And that's why we speak about dreams, and we'll engage in the journey of dreams and synchronicities as you work on your own Way Ahead projects. Here is a story from one of my former clients that illustrates this point:

My client had been brought up without any religion or talk of God. Her father, who she loved very much, had been a progressive, freethinker, humanist and atheist. Four years after his death, at a time when she was steeped in an existential crisis, unable to reconcile her own turmoil and the suffering in the world with the idea of "God," she had a dream. In the dream, her father was sliding down the rail of a stairway, wearing a top hat, and playfully waving a cane. When he hit the first floor he began to dance like

Fred Astaire. The woman was filled with joy to see her father and she asked him, "Father, is there life after death?"

> He smiled and said, "Of course there is! What do you think, we go through all this and then there is nothing?"

> She asked, "So what is there after death?"

> He smiled again and said: "For that you'll have to be patient and find out for yourself."

The phone message that woke her up from the dream announced that a spiritual teacher from India was coming to New York for three weeks to give talks on the philosophy of meditation, and the first night was "tonight." She went that night and every night thereafter for three weeks. The spiritual teacher spoke about karma—the cycle of cause and effect, about life and death and reincarnation, and the importance of finding a daily spiritual practice. But more importantly, the spiritual teacher gave my former client the experience of love and transcendence that took her beyond her skeptical mind, to the experience of the Self, the experience of the Collective Unconscious—the Tao.

That dream was a crossroads in this woman's life. She remembered it at times when her existential questioning nagged at her, and when life seemed pointless and hopeless. She continued to meditate and immerse herself in spiritual and esoteric studies. Today, over thirty years after that dream, she is a writer, teacher, healer, and uses the meditation methods she had learned from her teacher as a tool for transformation with her students and clients. That dream changed her life, in fact saved her life!

**Dreams are stories made up of images, symbols, words and sounds. They are portals to the Source. They deliver me sages and lessons, guidance, healing and prophecies.**

Sometimes we remember a dream clearly and entirely, as if it were written with a dramatic structure in mind, with character and plot and a problem that is resolved or not resolved. At other times the dream is lodged into our memory as only abstract, jumbled, intangible fractions, or blurs of color, sound and emotion. In either case, the dream possesses a feeling tone that every person who has ever had a nightmare or a supernatural dream will understand.

In sleep, fantasy takes the form of dreams, but in waking life one continues to dream just beneath the threshold of consciousness— expressing the ego, and the Shadow and Light of both the personal and Collective Unconscious. Any part of a dream can be used as a starting point. Active Imagination can be cultivated and practiced any time any place. By adding imagery or names, by expressing it in art or music or dance or writing, the dream is carried further; it can extend backwards or into the future. Dreams and fantasy, the awareness of synchronicities in our daily life, the power of the imagination—all play a key role in Way Ahead. This is a way of life. Any thought or deed that arises in the process is a production of your unconscious already designing your future. All you have to do is listen and take the next step.

INNER ATTITUDE

THE WESTERN APACHE MIND

# CHAPTER SIX

# THE WESTERN APACHE MIND

## THE RESERCH STAGE

*"Fate, character, innate image... together they make up the 'acorn theory,'*

*which holds that each person bears a uniqueness that asks to be lived*

*and that is already present before it can be lived."*

*~ James Hillman*

Way Ahead is not a "how to" formula for achieving a particular goal, like starting a business or finding a life partner, but rather it is a way of life. A creative and imaginative way of life! We identify our past and present numinous events and harness the psychological, cultural, artistic and spiritual components embedded in them toward creating a more pleasing and harmonious future. It is also the recognition that we are part of a world that we are constantly creating, and in the process the world creates and recreates us. We are in the world and the world is in us—we are not separate. "What we do to the Web, we do to ourselves," is a basic principal of all indigenous cultures. Our personal lives, our communities, and the planet are all intertwined in an endless play of giving and receiving. This is the way of the universe rearranges itself; when it's in harmony, it is in the right Tao. Way Ahead requires a similar holistic approach. We are being asked to bring the Tao back into balance.

## The Research

Like the Western Apache, we begin designing our Way Ahead with research. To conduct the research we follow the Western Apache approach, holding an attitude of smoothness, resilience, and steadiness of mind. With a smooth, resilient and steady mind we clean our windows of perception and take a look at our lives as if from the distance of a Satellite circling the earth. Like the early alchemists, we organize our research elements in terms of opposites. The inevitable attraction between opposites will lead to their eventual conjunction and, ultimately, to the creation of a new substance that arises out of, but is different from, the original substance. As researchers of our own lives we identify the opposites within us, our Shadow material, our projections, the mythological stories within our psyche, and the unconscious elements in our past significant events.

We do not yet evaluate or analyze our findings, we do not judge them, we just observe our past and our present, the defining moments in our lives, both simple and numinous, the events that shaped us, that carved the twists and turns on the many paths we've taken, or have taken us. We notice the surprising, unexpected and unavoidable holes we fell into, and the peak experiences in which we wanted to forever stay. We let images of our parents and grand

and great parents float on the screen of our consciousness, we hear the "voices" of neighbors and friends far and close, and of teachers, allies and enemies. We remember the joy of grace-filled moments of success and jubilation, and the contracted feelings of those times when we could not see or wanted to see, tomorrow.

The Western Apache attitude is not a step by step process but rather a playful contemplation that can be done anywhere, anytime, in the shower, while driving a car, seeing a film, or reading a book. Once we've imputed a question, an idea, a thought, into our mind, our subconscious mind has pulled it in and is already masticating it, even if we stop consciously thinking about it. It's a waking daydream. And like children who fantasize, who look up at the clouds, and then suddenly get up and create a cardboard rocket... so do we, get swept by the muse of creativity. A writer friend of mine told me that when she gets stuck in her writing she goes to her meditation cushion, sets an alarm clock for ten or fifteen minutes without thinking about her writing. Once the alarm goes on she returns to the computer, and babooom! The writing just flows. Often, while still in meditation, and before the alarm clock goes on, solutions to her writing problems begin to surface like oil on water, but she forces herself to wait for the alarm to go on before returning to her computer. That's her way. Each of us will find our own way to invoke our creativity and imagination using the Apache Wisdom attitude.

As we research our psyches, we inadvertently stumble on times in our lives—moments, hours, days—when we were shattered to pieces; a breakup from a lover, the death of a loved one, an unrealized creative project. This is an opportunity to recognize these pieces as the split off parts of ourselves that together create who we are today. Like a Japanese vase that had been broken and then the pieces were glued back up together in gold leaf. The value of such a vase in Japan is much higher than its value before it was broken.

Taking a satellite view of our psyche's journey, as well as scrutinizing specific moments, we see the hologram of our lives. It's important to recognize and celebrate the parts in us that are in balance with the Tao, the times when we felt whole and content. That will strengthen and help us heal and recover the parts in us that are not.

One of the founding elders of the Jungian project was Joe Henderson. When he was at a crossroads in his early life, just entering medical school, he had a dream. Many years later, in analysis, he understood the dream as a hologram that depicted his whole life from beginning to end. He understood it as an initiation journey. He had to pass through the ordeals of death, rebirth and renewal. A preparation journey we must all encounter and successfully navigate before we can proceed on and renew. On our return from this passage, we are often showered with gifts, such as renewed passion, insight and clarity, wisdom and even prophesy. This is what emerges out of this encounter with the deeper layer of the psyche, an initiation journey familiar to the indigenous tribes of today and earlier cultures.

## Tao & the 10,000 Things

9/11 was a rite of passage for America, and so are the traumatic events in our personal lives and the unhealed traumas in the lives of our parents, ancestors, communities and culture. Native Americans still carry the pain of Genocide inflicted on their ancestors, centuries ago. The psyches and bodies of African Americans still feel the pain of tight metal shackles around their ankles and wrists. The Jews have not yet healed the traumas of the Holocaust; the

Palestinians still suffer their own catastrophe—as a result. At the same time these are also the fabric of which art is made. Picasso's Guernica depicting the bombing of a Spanish village by Nazi and Fascist Italian planes and Tolstoy's novel War and Peace charting Napoleon's invasion of Russia, are but two examples. Crossing the planet north and south, east and west, we find remarkable works of art and literature, music and dance, film and theater born of genocide and atrocities, all rooted in various forms of pain and suffering. Does art heal? Who could tell? But the proof is in the pudding—a traumatic event is a crossroads—a hub of creativity and possibilities.

We can follow the trauma and spiral downward, or we can recognize the opportunity for healing, for change, for breakthrough, we can become the Wounded Healers of our times, for ourselves and for our surroundings. Mahatma Gandhi, Martin Luther King and Nelson Mandela had suffered unspeakable traumas, personal and collective, yet they found the courage and disciplined insight to turn hate into love and aggression into non-violent resistance. Each one of them had his own way through, for Gandhi it was meditation, for Martin Luther King it was prayer and the blues, for Mandela it was forgiveness and reconciliation.

At the crossroads we are forced to take inventory of the choices, and the choice-less choices, we have made. Were did we err? Did we err? Could we have chosen otherwise? What are our limitations? Are they real or are they irrational beliefs? When did we break through our limitations? Where will we be if we surpass our preconceived limitations?

And further: what do our nighttime dreams tell us? What was our childhood dream? Our past successes? We begin to notice synchronicities and serendipities, we pay attention to the kind of people we meet, to the fragments of wisdom in books and films, to events in the world around us. We shuffle through it all, searching for our "North Star"—our GPS—that will lead us to our destination.

## How is Your Destiny Leading you to Your Destination?

One of my friends shared with me that she was going through a rough time financially and creatively. She was working on selling her screenplay, and her fears and insecurities and the taste of past failures numbed her. She felt frozen just at a time when she needed to network and make phone calls and send emails. Driving in her car one day, she found herself taking a different route from the one she usually took. She was all consumed with her crisis of confidence, so she turned on the radio. Before long, a song on the radio titled Crossroads began to play. It was advertising Eric Clapton's music festival titled Crossroads. To her amazement, a moment later, she saw from the window of her car a café named "Crossroads," and a block later a boutique named "Crossroads." She was filled with awe and humility at how the Universe was mirroring her state of mind. She also realized that she had taken another route from the one she usually took in that part of town. That was a hint. Take another route! Go in the opposite direction! She began to apply this to her work. She dropped her fears, and instead began to market her screenplay with confidence and detachment. Like the Bhagavad Gita suggests: "Do you work, and don't get attached to the fruit of your work."

The Western Apache research stage echoes this detachment; it speaks about "drinking the nourishing waters"—and that's what she did. She could have just passed by all those "Crossroads" signs and say, "Oh what a coincidence," and forget the whole thing. But she trusted her gut, took it in and drank from the nourishing waters....

The Western Apache of the American Southwest have a rich medicine and expressive culture, filled with stories and ceremonies. The shaman not only suggests that we consider life as multidimensional, but offers distinct practices in order to experience this multidimensionality. Our conversation is not only by the use of words with someone in front of us or on the phone or by text, but with the totality of the 10,000 things. This is how we ease our way into living in the right Tao—we recognize our interconnectedness with all things and all beings.

## Daimon—the GPS at the Crossroads

It's important to recognize what motivates us, what makes us feel that we are at the right time and place and all is well in our lives. But often we work hard and our tree remains fruitless. This is when we need to ask ourselves whether our ladder is placed next to the right wall, or are we barking up the wrong tree?

What I called "our GPS," (Global Positioning Satellite) the Greeks called Daimon. It is our internal engine, unique to each one of us—an undeniable force that steers us on the tracks of destiny toward the intended destination of our soul. The term Daimon comes from Greek and means "replete with knowledge," or "divine power," "fate" or "god." The Greek philosopher Plato suggested that our Daimon—in other words, who we are meant to become—is given to us before we are ejected into this world. In the book The Soul's Code, James Hillman suggests that the Daimon itself selects a pattern or image or myth that must be lived out. The Greek teacher and philosopher Socrates said that he had a lifetime Daimon that always warned him of danger and bad judgment. He said his Daimon was more accurate than such omens as watching the flights or reading the entrails of birds, which were two respected forms of divination of the time. Unfortunately, in our scientifically modern, consumer culture, the Daimon has been forced underground by most, and the recognition and ability to listen to it has atrophied.

But my friend at the crossroads marketing her script has not lost the ability to listen to it.

Prone to human vulnerabilities, she asked herself if her work was good enough to sell in Hollywood or the international market. Was she not too old for this career? Would an agent pick her for representation? In other words, was she barking up the right tree?

To get some answers she pulled out cards from several divination cards—Tarot, Native American animal, and Goddess cards—one card from each deck. Two of the cards she pulled were number 19. When she glanced at the calendar she surprisingly noticed that the next day was July 19—a day that held special meaning for her as it was Guru Purnima—the full moon in July, the largest and brightest full moon of the year—celebrated on her spiritual path and all over India and Nepal as the bond between human and divine. Then my friend realized that the last draft of her script was dated May 19. And a passage from an Isabel Allende novel she loved, read, "You will have a lot of money... you will make it without effort, play number 19." Finally my friend remembered that 19 was the age when a traumatic event had occurred in her life, an event that set her on her life's path as a writer and healer, and was also connected to her screenplay. With all this feedback from the universe—all these synchronicities—she felt more confident on her journey of marketing her script. She felt that her Daimon was behind her, steering her, assuring her she was on the right track. Her GPS was well tuned!

## The Western Apache Attitude

Our state of mind affects everything we do. It is equally as important as our talent and great ideas, and some say even more. A great talent will be stifled and wilt away by a negative, neurotic attitude, while a lesser talent will quietly blossom into unexpected greatness with a healthy attitude. Creating your Way Ahead asks of you to hold the Western Apache attitude. Its triangle of wisdom lays the three fundamental virtues: smoothness, resilience and steadiness of mind.

## Smoothness of Mind

A smooth mind is as unruffled as a calm sea. It has a uniform consistency of motion and flow, devoid of abrupt curves. It is a smooth ride. No rough unexpected twists, turns, earthquakes or floods. Such smoothness of mind creates clarity, intuitive thinking, and a mental capacity to detect and avoid threatening circumstances when none are yet apparent. The smooth mind looks through events, deeply, beneath the surface, to discover the probabilities and possibilities.

Our minds create our reality. Imagine that
you approach everything in your life with
a smooth mind. How will it be?

## Resilience of Mind

A resilient mind has the power to return to its original, healthier form, after being hurt or broken. It has the ability to recover quickly from illness, depression, chaos, havoc and horrifying circumstances. It is buoyant and flexible, it does not fight or resent reality, it accepts WHAT IS and derives energy from this choice in creating a better future. The resilient mind maintains its ability to reason clearly—even under great duress.

Imagine yourself rise from the ashes of

pain and suffering with greater authentic

force and power than ever before.

This is resilience.

## Steadiness of Mind

A steady mind ensures its own immovability and authentic values similar to a hole in the ground that holds a stake firmly. To achieve this state, it is imperative to overcome aggressive tendencies toward others and relinquish thoughts of advantage, dominance, and supremacy. It is imperative to overcome narcissistic motivations and self-serving needs. Holding a steady mind—unimpeded by arrogance, pride, anger, vindictiveness, jealously or lust—is necessary in creating your Way Ahead.

Imagine how you would feel and act if
you were to hold a steady mind in the
face of any obstacle. The obstacle would
dissolve. Pfff into thin air!

These three mental conditions produce wisdom—the instrument of future survival. This is practical wisdom, similar to the fluid movement of water and its life-nourishing qualities. The more the defining moments in our lives are recognized as resources for inspiration, and the more we cultivate the ability to drink and be nourished by the 10,000 things, the deeper our wisdom. The courage to engage with the unconscious and its archetypal phenomena and to maintain the exploratory qualities of shamans is vital in Way Ahead. Vital to sailing across both calm and stormy waters...

This attitude resembles what Freud and Jung named Creative Illnesses. Or what is known as the Wounded Healer, or the adage "the wisdom is in the wound." This attitude often gifts us with "mana"—the gift of the gods—an undeniable authentic power. Often this gift is the outcome of the suffering and breaking through the dry desert valleys in our lives, which we crossed with great fear that didn't stop us, and then reached an oasis...

Much of our story has been lived automatically, unconsciously, like doodling on a paper tablecloth at a restaurant. Yet, many of us have already done deep conscious healing work and have recognized our Daimon—our inner GPS—that has been navigating us thus far. In Way Ahead, whether for the first time or the hundred's time, we update our psyche to align and realign with our archetypal model, in harmony with the Tao.

## This is no Ordinary Research—this is Self Research

To launch our Way Ahead, like the Western Apache, we start with research. This research is an experience in deepening and expanding our awareness. We become aware of our lives and souls, and we come to understand, remember, forgive, and in some cases even detach from our old stories that no longer serve us. However in many cases the "old" stuff lingers and continues to haunt. Allow this to be, allow this haunting to come into view, into your mind's eye, allow these memories to trickle up to the surface like oil trapped in the earth below. Often, just allowing the memories to emerge will release the hidden power they have over you. What may follow is forgiveness and letting go of past traumas—vital components in the process of healing and transformation.

Following is a list of topics—call them fields—in which you can let your mind roam, travel and discover. You can write down your thoughts, you can draw them, or dance or sing the feelings they evoke in you. You can speak to a trusted friend about them, or contemplate those memories and images as you drive your car or take a shower or before you go to sleep. You will be roaming in the field of your heart. In what has seemed to be a random, arbitrary, wild field you will begin to discern a path. Your path!

Let us be inspired by Joseph Campbell who wrote:

You enter the forest at the darkest point,

where there is no path. Where there is a

way or path, it is someone else's path.

You are not on your own path. If you follow
someone else's way, you are not going
to realize your potential.

The mythologist Joseph Campbell was a masterful storyteller. He could weave tall tales from every corner of the world into spellbinding narratives. His lifelong quest from childhood days as a devout Catholic altar boy to fame as the world's most noted scholar in comparative mythology makes for a grand and heroic story.

### 1.    *The place of your birth*

The language spoken; the political regime (democracy, theocracy, war zone, etc.), the weather; the landscape of your childhood (mountain, the sea, a river rolls by, etc.). Important events that took place in that landscape. Those are just examples—please add your own thoughts and memories. This goes for the all the next topics.

### 2.    *Your parents*

Their age at your birth. Their economic, ethnic and religious background. Their attitudes toward life (optimistic? Hopeful? Generous?) The lessons you learned from you parents, teachers, neighbors and friends—those that served you and still do, and those you wish to unlearn. Behaviors you observed as a child in your surroundings (alcoholism, religion, art, politics)

### 3.    *Your culture and religion or non-religion*

The demands of your culture or religion (the obligation to get married; follow your father's footsteps in business, etc.) The rules you followed and those you rebelled against.

### 4.    *The meaningful events that happened to you at 3 at 6 at 9 at 10*

Divorce, immigration, illness, death, or abandonment of any kind. Support and love you were showered with. War, occupation or political upheaval. Your best friends at the time. Influential books, films and TV series that affected you. Trips to other countries, cities, or in nature.

### 5.    *Turning points in your life*

The meaningful events that happened to you at the crossroads and the choices you made. The choices that were made for you!

### 6.    *Your gifts—things you are good at*

In business, vocation, relationships with family, friends and romantic partners.

### 7.    *Things that motivate you to get out of bed in the morning*

Food, meditation, running, writing, hurrying to a job you love or not love. The beautiful faces of your children, your spouse, your pet, your garden, your art.

### 8.    *Your hopes, dreams and wishes for your future*

Imagine how you will feel when those are fulfilled.

**9.** *Your contributions to others*

The feeling you experienced when you supported and helped other people. Would you like to contribute more to yourself and others? How can you do this?

**10.** *Three memorable nighttime dreams you had*

If you followed them, recall where they led you. If you did not follow them—what was the outcome of that?

**11.** *Three memorable synchronicities*

There is a divine thread interwoven in the fabric of your life. Can you see it?

This is the landscape of your life as you know it. Become aware of its many pathways and crossroads, honor yourself, your struggles and your successes, and let the lessons lead you onward and upward. Plow the soil of the field but don't dig too harshly into it—the answers and the questions will come to you naturally in their own time.

As the novelist and poet Maria Rilke tells us:

Be patient toward all that is unsolved

in your heart and try to love the questions

themselves, like locked rooms and

like books that are now written in a

very foreign tongue. Do not now seek

the answers, which cannot be given you

because you would not be able to live them.

And the point is, to live everything.

Live the questions now.  Perhaps you will

then gradually, without noticing it,

live along some distant day into the answer.

KEYSTONE PRACTICE

JOURNALING

# CHAPTER SEVEN
# SMALL CHANGES
## BIG RESULTS

*A keynote practice is like a rudder on a ship that with the slightest turn will shift the course of a voyage...*

In Way Ahead, the keystone practice is journaling. Journaling grants us two boons—one is of a psycho-spiritual nature, the other is practical. Keeping a journal is a direct and immediate connection to our unconscious, to uncovering and healing our deep self, to discovering things about ourselves which lay beneath our conscious, thinking, cerebral mind. At the same time it is also a journey towards mastery, working practically through what the unconscious is revealing to us, continually improving and clarifying our thoughts and actions in the world. With the unconscious being the wellspring in Way Ahead, you can see why journaling would be so invaluable to it.

## Goals, Intentions and Resolutions

How many of us have made goals in the past, particularly around the New Year, only to see them crumble away? There is a tendency in human nature that when trying to change something, we try to change everything. But with modern life being as busy and demanding as it is, straining to tackle our list of resolutions all at once—going to the gym, starting a diet, organizing our office, signing up to an Internet dating service, and so on—we tackle nothing. Without a plan or direction on how to incorporate these naturally and easily into our lives, we drop them quite immediately or they fall by the wayside on their own. And understandably so—it's just too much to do! Often our resolutions do not even represent our own authentic needs but rather a societal imposition such as dieting or dating—so no wonder they fall away. Our resolutions may also be tremendously inflated, fantasies that will never ever see the light of day because they are just too grand and not grounded in the earth. Every tree must have soil and water to nourish it into continual life ... thus, such resolutions are doomed to dry up.

Another reason for the crumbling of our resolutions and intentions is that something in our unconscious prevents them from being realized. Somewhere in our unconscious there is a past failure in the same or similar area, a painful experience we could not face—which is how it ended up in the darkness of our unconscious in the first place. Until we become aware of that painful past experience and heal it, we might be walking up a steep hill in realizing our current goals.

Our failed goals and intentions, conscious and unconscious, are exhausting and frustrating. As a result, we begin to find all the things that are wrong with us, with our lives and with our New

Year resolutions. It's called self-sabotage. We say, "I like food too much so this diet is not for me," or "the gym is too far away and too expensive," or "I am not attracted to anyone on the Internet dating site." Excuses, excuses ... So we run to a therapist in the hope that he or she will solve our problems, only to end up in more loss and despair and ultimately burn out.

## The Kaizen Process

An effective approach, and one that saves us from unrealistic and sabotaging behaviors, is to take the time and work on current, authentic personal needs and goals that will change and transform our life into the one we dream and wish it to be. It is wise to find a point of departure—a keystone habit that strengthens and anchors our positive intentions and behaviors. This keystone habit is also where we return to in the stormier days of life.

Let us take the example of the Kaizen Process—a keystone habit that was used in Japan to build an automobile empire—the Toyota enterprise.

Kaizen is the Japanese word for "improvement," or "change for better." When used in the business sense and applied to the work-place, Kaizen refers to one or more ongoing, small incremental changes that potentially affect every element in the production and financial chain. Kaizen was first implemented in Japan after World War II, influenced partly by American business and quality management. Since then it has been applied in healthcare, psychotherapy, life coaching, government, banking and other industries. The process also stresses a humanized approach to workers, based on the fact that when people are sincerely acknowledged and respected they'll give their best to create the finest product.

The following is a good example: a movie set is an environment in which many egos often butt heads—which in turn interferes with the progress and success of the creative work. On one such movie set, a producer established a rule among the crew and cast: no matter what happened in the workday, when they call "wrap" they all shake hands with each other, smile and say "Thank you." And guess what? This small action had a profound positive effect on productivity. When an upset arose, the mere remembrance of the handshake agreement automatically loosened workers' egos, and civilized communication replaced grievances, yelling and hurt. A simple gesture can go a long way...

The Kaizen principal applies to every component in a company, from the CEO to the assembly line workers. Small changes and new habits, when introduced into daily, weekly and monthly routines, will inevitably improve and advance the entire system. Small changes produce big results. Like in aviation. A slight change of angle in the incipient point of departure will divert the trajectory of a plane from flying to Paris to flying to Rio de Janeiro.

You might start eating a healthy breakfast every morning and unknowingly begin taking the stairs at the office instead of the elevator, becoming more dynamic at work as a result. You begin taking hikes in the local mountains on the weekends and suddenly you have more empathy toward your colleagues and significant others. You manage to avoid spontaneous impulsive purchases, as a result you feel more at ease and less stressed, and suddenly your motivation toward your New Year's resolutions and other goals has increased. The previous, deeply ingrained patterns in your brain have begun to dissolve and reform, and you have become an entirely different human being—instead of a human doing.

## All because you started having a healthy breakfast every morning!

### Journaling

As mentioned above, our keystone practice in Way Ahead—our own Kaizen—is journaling. Journaling daily and being rigorous about doing exactly that, is like having a healthy breakfast every morning. As you follow the guidelines presented in this chapter and develop and assimilate the practice into your daily life, you will show up enhanced in every area requiring focused creative attention. This small but mighty practice will change everything!

Many people have tried and failed at journaling or done it for a few months and then stopped, never to pick it up again. The need to journal usually peaks during periods of deep change, when we are at a crossroads, experiencing extreme emotional pain or joy and we can no longer hold it all inside, so we pick up our journal and pour our hearts out into it. Career change, relationship breakup, the birth of a child or the death of a loved one are but a few examples. At such times the unconscious is deeply activated and one may become flooded with thoughts and imagery that you "download" onto your journal. But when these crossroads have been traversed, the journaling stops. The key is to keep journaling. This is Kaizen: small, consistent, ongoing improvements every day of your life.

## The Way Ahead Method of Journaling

As you've read so far, Way Ahead engages the unconscious in recreating our lives. The most potent time for the unconscious to be active and undisturbed by the musings of the day is when we are asleep. Therefore, in the Way Ahead method, our day begins at night before we go to sleep.

When the conscious mind is asleep, our unconscious speaks to us through dreams. It is the time for our night sea journey. Even if we don't remember the dreams, and many of us do not, they will echo in the morning and for the rest of the day in the form of insights or creative impulses.

We journal three times a day: before we go to sleep at night, when we wake up in the morning, and at the end of the workday. (Those who work at night, please adjust this method to fit your schedule).

## Before going to bed at night write in your journal for 10 minutes

Thomas Edison said, "Never go to sleep without a request to your subconscious." Our first journal entry of each day is to speak to our unconscious before we go to sleep, tell it our joys and our sorrows. Tell it our needs and also our gratitude. For example: "I need to wake up early tomorrow morning and write ten page in my dissertation. I ask you, dear unconscious, please give me a dream in the night that will evoke my creativity in the morning," or, "please let me wake up with new and innovative ideas for my dissertation," or, "thank you dear unconscious for the dream about the screaming woman—it affirmed my work on a chapter on emotional upheaval I was describing in my dissertation—thank you so much again!" It is a good thing to address the unconscious with terms of endearment and not demand or force it to answer us or do anything for us.

It is perfectly wise to tell your unconscious, in writing, what specific areas in your life or in your work you're struggling with. Or what good ideas you have and ask for "feedback." The more specific the questions, the clearer will be the images emerging from your nocturnal dreaming or the insights and ideas surfacing the following days.

> The unconscious always answers.
>
> That is its job. You just have to listen.
>
> But like in any relationship, it's important
>
> to create a space for it to emerge into,
>
> and that is your journal.

If you'd like, you can meditate before or after your journaling. In this way you become closer and more available to your unconscious and your unconscious to you. If you are not a meditator, you can just sit quietly with yourself for a few minutes, close your eyes and focus on your breath—the way it comes in and goes out on its own. When your mind wanders, bring your attention back to the breath... it's as simple as that...

Journaling in the Way Ahead method connects you with your unconscious and is similar to what Carl Jung coined Active Imagination. Both are alchemical processes that integrate sets of fragmented and dissociated parts into a third whole.

*Figure 7: L0076403 Anonymous, Wellcome Library, London. The image on the left of the crowned male seated in the vessel below burning parts of the body bears the inscription: "Lors fut le roy esleue de Couronne des couronnel[s]' (Then was the King elected crown of the crowns' 15th century.*

Way Ahead is a caldron in which our guck and our luster are mixed, and in the mix are turned into a new and improved substance. And why is it so? No one wakes up one day and starts this cauldron. Something in our life goes wrong and is the catalyst for this process—the fire underneath the cauldron that causes the bubbling, evaporation and creation of the new substance. Something in our lives goes wrong and urges us to change, to transform.

## Night Journey Intentions

When you close your eyes, and before you fall asleep, remember your journal entry and hold in your consciousness the questions and your goals for the next day. These are your bedtime intentions.

For example, as I close my eyes to go to sleep at night, I silently tell myself: "I am waking up at 7:00AM, write for 10 minutes in my journal, go for a walk, have a healthy breakfast. Then I write for four hours and am greatly inspired. The emails and phone calls I make regarding my business are spoken with confidence and kindness..." etc. Say them in the present tense, as if your intentions are already manifest. You will see how easily and successfully you will achieve your goals the following day. It is a way to "program" your mind toward doing these tasks! It is like rehearsing. There is a story about an Olympic skier, who, months before the Olympic Winter Games, goes to the ski slope where he will be competing and he skis there. Then, back at his home, he practices skiing as if he were there—on the slope of the Olympic Winter Games location. This is how he "programs" his mind toward success.

## When you wake up in the morning, journal for 10 minutes

Research confirms that the brain, specifically the prefrontal cortex, is most active and readily creative immediately following sleep. Your unconscious mind has been on its night sea journey while you slept, making connections between the material and non-material worlds. These connections are available to you upon awakening—and it's easy to put them into words or creative shapes right then and there.

In a recent interview, former chess prodigy and tai chi world champion Josh Waitzkin explains his morning routine to tap into the breakthroughs and connections provided by his unconscious while he was sleeping. Unlike so many of us who check our smartphones within fifteen minutes of waking up, Waitzkin goes to a quiet place, does some meditation and grabs his journal. Thus, rather than focusing on input, like emails and texts, social media and the news, Waitzkin's focus is on output. In his journal, he "thought-dumps"—as he calls it—for several minutes. This is how he taps into his higher realms of clarity, learning and creativity: first by "dumping" his thoughts onto the paper, which in turn leads him to a "crystallized intelligence."

The writer Dorothea Brande is another example. As way back as 1934, decades before brain research discovered the role of the right and left-brain in all human endeavors, Brande was teaching her students in creative writing how to call forth the "inner writer." Her work is described in her book "Becoming a Writer." One of the key instructions she gives in the book is to write first thing upon waking up, before brushing one's teeth or taking a shower, before the cup of coffee. That time, when one is no longer asleep but not yet fully awake, is the time when the muses strike!

A friend of mine had an experience of the power of sleep—and a dream—to inspire her work. She was a film student writing and directing a short film, and could not figure out a particular scene. Frustrated, she decided to take a nap in the middle of the day. In her sleep she had a dream, and when she woke up she realized it was the exact scene she needed! My friend and her film crew shot the scene frame by frame as she had dreamt it.

Our nighttime sleep is the interval from one day to the next, the time our ideas are germinating in the fertile soil of the unconscious.

Whether you can remember your dreams or not upon awakening, you have been dreaming! Your mind is potent with the creative nutrients infused into it while you were asleep, and you don't want to waste the freshness of that new growth. So pick up your journal and start writing!

Consider the requests or questions you posed to your unconscious just before you went to sleep. What answers are you getting? What did you dream? Write it down. If you feel that you are not getting any answer, and do not remember your dreams, then jot down whatever image or thought comes to your mind. That will take you forward.

From time to time, you can use the non-dominant hand to write in your morning journal. In doing so you'll be using the right side of the brain, the part that is more intuitive and able to write down a dream or a thought or a memory without your more analytical left brain jumping in to interpret, judge or analyze it. That will come later.

Sometimes we wake up anxious or in a bad mood. Write your feelings down. It is the "thought dumping" stage, as Josh Waitzkin named it. When your mind becomes clearer and you're more at east, you might hear the answers to your questions and remember the dreams your unconscious has brought up.

Often after "thought dumping" my mind becomes calmer and I get ideas for articles I'm going to write. I get ideas about how I can be a better husband and father. I get clarity about the goals I am pursuing. I get insights about people I need to connect with, or how I can improve my current relationships.

The morning journal is also the time to make our "to do" lists and intentions for the day. I recommend having only a few items to start with. It is better to have fewer goals and accomplish all of them, rather than have too many and fall short. This will fortify your accountability to yourself and others.

Mental creation always precedes physical creation. Before a building is physically constructed, there's a blueprint. And before the blueprint is drawn there's an idea, a thought. Sometimes the entire completed building will appear in a dream way before it is being worked on in reality. In such a case, the dreamer will be permeated with the purpose and strength to pursue the project, because on some level—the building is already up and standing!

You are the participant in the design of your destiny and your thoughts are the blueprint of the life you are building one day at a time. When you learn to make friends with your mind you create the conditions that make the achievement of your goals possible. The simple routine of journaling will help you crystallize where you want to go, and how to go about it. It will open up energetic pathways in your brain and in your world that you cannot even conceive of in your every day busy mind!

"A human cannot directly choose the circumstances, but they can choose their thoughts, and so indirectly, yet surely, shape future circumstances."

~ James Allen

**At the end of your workday, write for 10 minutes in your journal**

These 10-minute sessions are designed so that you can become accountable for what you wanted to accomplish on this day. Did you accomplish all your goals? This would mean victory. And a personal, private victory precedes out-in-the-world public victory. Or, if you did not accomplish all that you had planned, what can be moved to tomorrow or the next week? And—most importantly— examine why you fell short on your goals: was it because you were too over optimistic? Was it too big a task? Or did you experience an internal resistance to performing a particular task, like make an important phone call or write an emotionally difficult email? Your journaling will reveal your inner workings, your resistances, your blocks, and your motivations.

The primary objective of this 10-minute after-work session is to mentally turn-off your day life—the way one refuels and recovers one's body after a workout. Think of it this way: last night you went out on a night sea journey, in the morning you came back to port and began your day; in the evening you returned to the port and are now reviewing your day's travels. After the 10-minute journaling it's the time to engage and be present with your family, your significant other, or your artistic passion. Rest and re-provision your ship for the next night's sea journey.

And now...


**... as one day has ended and a new one begins...**

**...go back to writing in your journal for 10 minutes before going to sleep ...**

Journaling daily, you are building up a habit of reading and re-writing your goal direction. Similar to sailing, you have charted a course, you know where you are going but the winds change daily, and sometimes there is no wind at all and you need to compensate. Journaling helps you "read the weather"—the signals emerging from your unconscious.

The pages of your journal become the navigating maps of your voyage—the building blocks for your future life—your Way Ahead. And furthermore, in this daily journaling process you are building a constant, accountable and trust worthy relationship with your unconscious. The more you will "be there" for it—the more the unconscious will be there for you.

## Your unconscious is your best friend and best teacher!

### Journaling Strengthens Gratitude

Even if you start a journaling session in a bad mood, the awareness that comes forth from writing has a subtle way of shifting your mind towards gratitude. Creativity is an antidote to depression and apathy—that's a well-known truth. And journaling can be creative. Not only what you write but the journal you write in, the little drawings you may add here and there, the desk you sit at, maybe you have a flower in front of you, or a candle, or an inspiring picture or object. Sometimes I pick up leaves along the paths I walk and place them into my journal. They remind me of the places I have been and the thoughts I was having at those times.

I know someone who worked out an entire stage production using journaling. Initially she would dump her fears and insecurities onto the page, and only when she felt empty of "muck" she proceeded to work on the characters' motivations and actions, the set design, music and so forth. Then she began to thank her journal for listening and giving good advice. The play was successful—her gratitude grew—and her journal became a Gratitude Journal.

So you can include gratitude in your daily journaling. When you start writing what you're grateful for, new perspectives of thought open up in the citadel of your mind. An attitude of gratitude will change your entire life orientation from scarcity to abundance. The world will increasingly become a more playful place. Your gratitude will turn you into a person worthy of the gratitude of others. You'll experience living in the cycle of giving and receiving.

"Gratitude unlocks the fullness of life. It turns what we have into enough, and more. It turns denial into acceptance, chaos to order, confusion to clarity. It can turn a meal into a feast, a house into a home, a stranger into a friend."
**~ Melody Beattie**

"Gratitude toward all our gifts is a practice that strengthens our connection to the web of life that supports us."
**~ Stephan David Hewitt**

Write in your journal for 30 days straight, three times a day... for journaling is the "small" but mighty element in the Way Ahead method that improves and clarifies our our lives!

## Journaling is our own Kaizan!

Like the Japanese that built a powerful automobile empire, you will build your own new life, using journaling as a way of clarifying your thoughts and actions toward mastery in the world. You will maintain the Western Apache attitude of smoothness, resilience and steadiness of mind, not only in the research stage but throughout the whole process of Way Ahead, and hopefully for the rest of your life.

EVALUATION

THE SCIENTIFIC METHOD

# CHAPTER EIGHT
# MIND FUSION

*"Science, my boy, is made up of mistakes, but they are mistakes which it is useful to make, because they lead little by little to the truth."*

*~ Jules Verne, Journey to the Center of the Earth*

*"No one, from pontiffs to professors, has a monopoly on the truth. In the end, we are all just travelers--not scientists or mystics or any one brand of thinker. By nature, we are scientists and mystics, reductionists and holists, left-brained and right-brained, mixed up creatures trying to catch an occasional glimpse of the truth. The best we can do is to be tolerant of both sides of our nature--knowing that these reflect the twin aspect of the universe—and learn from whatever wisdom is offered."*

*~ David Darling*

So far you've learned, practiced and cultivated three major components of Way Ahead: Jungian philosophy, the Apache Mind attitude, and journaling. You dreamed and envisioned and gave words and shapes to the ruminations of your mind and musings of your heart. You thought and pondered, meditated and contemplated—as you examined your past and your present seeking to understand the connections between events. You discovered the moments in your life when your natural talents had brought you joy and success as well as the moments in which you had suffered havoc and trauma. In this primary research you began to more clearly understand the story of your life. This work has been primarily right brain work, governed by your emotions, feelings, intuitions, desires, memories, reflections, perceptions and instincts. But there is a fourth major component to Way Ahead and to writing and applying the scenarios. This fourth component is the more reason-oriented methodology discovered by Rene Descartes, known as the Scientific Method.

It is through the sieve of the Scientific Method that we pass each of the three components, separately or combined. In this way we fuse right and left-brain, intuition and reason, the spiritual and the material, our personal destiny with the destiny of our community and the planet at large. This is the Tao of Way Ahead—learning to live in harmony with ourselves and with the spheres of life around us.

*Descartes says: I think, therefore I am.*

*Carl Jung's philosophy suggests: I love, I feel, therefore I am.*

*Way Ahead suggests balancing the two.*

## Descartes' Scientific Method

The Renaissance was one time in history that changed—you can say, "upgraded"—our world enormously. The biggest upgrade was the departure from blind faith in the church and its doctrines toward engaging in scientific discoveries that are reached and proven by scientific methods. The father of the Scientific Method was Rene Descartes—a French philosopher and mathematician. Fascinatingly, this method was conceived in a dream Descartes had.

In his dream Descartes was in a charged room on a stormy night filled with ghosts. There were sparks and sounds of thunder. There was another room beside this one, an empty peaceful room with only one object in it. A book! The book was open, with one line written in it that read, "What path shall I take?"

The following day, Descartes contemplated the dream. He understood the image of the open book and the single line written in it to be a calling for humankind to question one's life and the universe, implying the existence of free will and independent, personal choice. This became the Scientific Method. Here is what he wrote in his 1637 Discourse on the Method of Rightly Conducting the Reason and Seeking for Truth in the Sciences:

"Instead of the great number of precepts of which Logic is composed, I believed that I should find the four which I shall state quite sufficiently, provided that I adhered to a firm and constant resolve never on any single occasion to fail in their observance."

## 1. Doubt everything.

To accept nothing as true which I did not clearly recognize to be so.... to carefully avoid haste and prejudice in judgment... and to accept nothing more than what was presented to my mind clearly and distinctly.

## 2. Break every problem into smaller parts.

To divide up each of the difficulties examined into as many parts as possible.

## 3. Solve the simplest problems first.

To commence with objects that are the most simple and easy to understand in order to rise little by little, or by degrees, to the knowledge of the most complex.

## 4. Be thorough.

To make enumerations so complete, and reviews so encompassing, so as to be certain of having omitted nothing.

In 1638, Galileo Galilei applied Descartes' Scientific Method to support his own investigations into the nature of the universe and confirmed Copernicus's finding that the sun does not circle the earth, but the other way around. This was one gigantic "Way Ahead upgrade" for humankind!

By fusing all four components—Jungian philosophy, the Apache Mind attitude, journaling, and Descartes' Scientific Method we will leave our own "dark ages" and reach our personal renaissance. We might learn that we do not circle around society and its demands of us, but that in fact it is the opposite: society circles around us—around our own consciousness. And when we change our consciousness, life, the universe, society, everyone and everything will provide us with the means to achieve our hopes and dreams. For Way Ahead is work in consciousness!

### How to apply Descartes's Scientific Method to Way Ahead

1. Doubt everything you have been taught, and instead, seek to find your true calling and authentic needs. When you find your core—your spine—you begin to heal. This is a process, not a one-time event, and a fascinating one as such.

> **Maybe the journey is not so much about becoming anything. Maybe it is about un-be-coming everything that is not really you, so you can be who you were meant to be in the first place. ~ Anonymous**

2. Break every problem into smaller parts using your journal, your Apache Mind attitude, and all the Jungian principles you have learned.

For example: say you are writing a screenplay. It's a long and laborious process that can take years to complete even for the most accomplished screenwriters. Start by writing one or two or three sentences for what the script is about. Then figure out what the three acts are, and the turning points that move the story from one act to the next. Structure your script on 5-7 cards, and so on. Then, when you begin to actually write your script, give yourself a time limit for a writing session. I know a successful screenwriter who works from 10:00AM to 4:00PM every day, with the goal of writing four pages a day.

"Breaking something down into smaller chunks allows you to see more clearly how the pieces fit, and how to tackle each piece individually. Seeing its smaller components can often help get you started because now you have some-thing you can actually do." ~ Iris Shoor

3. Solve the simplest problem first suggests that you cannot go sailing around the world, for example, if your back hurts. First you must solve your back issues. Or, don't invest in a new business if you still owe alimony to your ex wife that you can hardly pay.

4. Be thorough... complete your cycles of action on all levels, do your best, be accountable to yourself and to others, keep your word and agreements, be courteous.

## The Fusion of Right and Left Brain Hemispheres

Research led by evolutionary anthropologist Dean Falk at Florida State University and released on October 4, 2013 found that Albert Einstein's brilliance might be linked to the fact that his brain hemispheres were extremely well connected. The ability to use right brain creativity and left-brain logic may have been what made Einstein a genius. So it was no coincidence that Einstein was a genius physicist and a master violinist. After having been inspired by the music of Mozart at age 13, he began to practice the violin religiously. Practicing an instrument engages the right and left-brain hemispheres and makes them more well-connected. More and more studies are beginning to link musical training and improved cognitive function.

Another example from Albert Einstein's life that might inspire us as we write our future scenarios is the following: Einstein loved to take long walks and ride his bicycle around Princeton University. He once said of E=mc2, "I thought of it while riding my bicycle." If you look at the daily routines of creative greats, there is a strong link between some type of bi-pedal aerobic motion that engages right and left-brain hemispheres that leads to Eureka moments and creative breakthroughs. Neuroscientific research points to the interconnection between right and left-brain hemispheres. So when you write your scenarios, take yourself for a walk and let the scenarios float in your mind informing you of the possibilities, or take a bath and daydream your future, or go write in the park or in a café. These changes in your habits will help create the interconnectedness between the right and left-brain. Or take meditation breaks when you feel stuck or need to be further inspired. Make the writing of the scenarios be a fun and pleasurable experience. Surprise yourself!

# YOUR THREE SCENARIOS

## THE PROBABLE

## THE PREFERABLE

## THE POSSIBLE

# CHAPTER NINE

# HOW TO WRITE THE THREE SCENARIOS AND WHICH ONE TO CHOOSE?

*"You can't connect the dots looking forward; you can only connect them looking backwards. So you have to trust that the dots will somehow connect in your future. You have to trust in something—your gut, destiny, life, karma, whatever. This approach has never let me down, and it has made all the difference in my life."*
*~ Steve Jobs*

*"If you think in terms of a year, plant a seed; if in terms of ten years, plant trees; if in terms of 100 years, teach the people."*
*~ Confucius*

We've come to the central stage of Way Ahead, which is writing the three scenarios. Our research, learning and practicing the Western Apache attitude, journaling, and the examination of our lives through the lens of the Scientific Method—have all been our preparation for this stage. Now is the time to funnel our discoveries, our dreams and goals, and our imagination into writing the three future scenarios and choose to live by one of them. So how do we do that?

It is important to remember that while Way Ahead is a system that will support you in starting and implementing any particular project—writing a book, initiating a new business, starting or healing a relationship, improving your health, and so on and so forth—it is much more than that. It is a philosophy, a way of life, an ecologically sound and holistic collaboration between heart, mind, body and spirit. It is a fluid dance in which each step moves us forward toward a healthier, happier, more successful, more compassionate life. It is a system that asks us to be flexible and trustworthy, imaginative, generous and courageous. It asks us to live outside the box and turn yesterday's doubts into tomorrow's brave actions. Primarily, first and foremost, and I cannot stress this enough, it is work in consciousness, and as such, it is true magic—for magic starts with raising our consciousness—and I am not speaking about magic as in pulling a rabbit out of a hat. I am speaking about raising our consciousness so as to perceive and understand even our direst moments as opportunities for growth, for learning and transformation. And in this way, we can indeed pull a rabbit out of a hat...

The seeds—or shall I say, the "applications"—of your DesitnyOS are your dreams and intuitions, your lifelong desires and wishes, the synchronicities and serendipities you've experienced, your talents and gifts, your personal, social and professional relationships, and your successes and failures. Yes, failures too, are essential to review and to learn from, for they will reveal to you not only your weaknesses and vulnerabilities but also your strength of heart and resilience.

**Your new Way Ahead is embedded in the old one. It is its point of departure, its home, like the capsule is the home of a rocket launched into space.**

As Steven Jobs said: "You can't connect the dots looking forward; you can only connect them looking backwards. So you have to trust that the dots will somehow connect in your future." They will connect, in the same way that a ripe fruit will fall from a tree because it's ready to start the next cycle. And because causes create effects and nothing goes to waste in this universe of ours. So it's important to see and understand your life story and the trajectory it has taken to this point—so as to actively imagine and pave the path toward your future.

## The Four Components for Writing the Scenarios—a Short Review

## Jungian Philosophy

Like the nucleus of an atom, the core of Way Ahead is the Jungian philosophy, which we explored in chapters 2 to 5. This is the central and most essential part of the work and influences every movement in the process and every particle of your evolution. Like the nucleus of an atom—that possesses the positively charged proton and the neutron that is of the same mass but without the electric charge—Jungian philosophy values the marriage of opposites, the Light and the Shadow, the depths as well as the surfaces.

## The Western Apache Attitude

As introduced in chapter 6, you are invited to hold the Western Apache attitude in each step of the way as you design your future and live your life: smoothness, resilience and steadiness of mind. Of course, being human, you'll surely "lose it" or become "inflated" from time to time. When this happens, become aware of your feelings and accept the situation without judgment, reconnect to your inner GPS, rebalance, and resume the Western Apache attitude. In other words, get back on the horse...

CAUTION! Often we are not capable of accepting "what is" without judgment, it just can't be done! It is important to become aware of the triggers and bring into relevance your emotional world. It will give you guidance as to which route to take next. Think of that pit of fear in your stomach when you are about to Bungee jump off a bridge. This is your feeling function and should be used as your ongoing guide. Bring full awareness to what you like and don't like.

## Journaling

In chapter 7, we spoke about a keystone practice—the one simple daily practice that is a game changer—and you were advised to make that practice, journaling. This means recording your dreams and intentions, your fears and joys, your winning and losing moments.

## The Scientific Method

The fourfold method: Doubt everything. Break every problem into smaller parts. Solve the simplest problems first. Be thorough.

## Writing the Three Scenarios

I invite you to imagine your life as a field. You have plowed and fertilized the soil in preparation to writing the three future scenarios for your life: the Probable, Preferable and Possible. You have options. You can plant the same kind of seeds you've been planting all along and reap a similar crop, sometimes not a very happy one—often an unfortunate one. Or, you can plant new seeds that have the potential to solve world hunger, but such seeds have never before been sown in your plot of land and the risk is enormous: you may end up hungry and bankrupt. Or, you can fuse the two options: that which you know and that which you are willing to take a risk on, but not at the risk of your survival.

To put it in the simplest of terms: the first scenario is continuation, the second scenario is your best hopes, and the third one is the golden path in between.

Soon you will begin to write these down, considering what you want to plant in each plot of land so as to realize the harvest you envision reaping. Your unconscious is already working on this—overtime—I promise you!

In describing the process of writing each of the scenarios I will include dreams by a few masters of Science and Art and discuss how these masters were guided by their dreams in the creation of their lives' work. I will always remind you, invite you, and cajole you to pay attention to your own dreams and to make them an integral part of your life—a motivating, guiding force. I will illuminate the important elements to consider in the writing of each scenario, and I will give additional tools to be applied.

## Scenario A· The Probable (continuation)

In the introduction to the book, I wrote about Cultural Futuristics and the three scenarios I had written as potential outcomes of the September 11, 2001 attacks on the World Trade Center in New York City. In thinking about the Probable Scenario following that unfathomable event, I was reminded of Albert Einstein's insight, that, "No problem can be solved from the same level of consciousness that created it." Sadly, I realized, the US government did just that: it tried to solve the problem with the same consciousness that had created it, thus continuing Islamophobia, militarism, oil addiction, and worse. This was the Probable Scenario for 9/11. Inertia.

In writing your Probable Scenario, you'll describe what your life will be like if you continue to do what you are already doing. In other words: if you do not consciously make any substantial changes in your material or nonmaterial life, or if the changes are so small they are almost invisible and non-effective. This is perfectly fine if you are satisfied with your life as it is and you don't feel the necessity for major change. At the very least, by writing down the life-scenario you choose to continue living you'll be making your fate conscious, exposing what has been lived unconsciously, making the unconscious, conscious. You'll be getting to know yourself better. You'll recognize your strengths and weaknesses and take responsibility for areas in your life you feel you have erred toward yourself or others. With responsibility will come acceptance, followed by a release of the old and emergence of the new.

Merely writing the Probable Scenario—which will not describe a major change but a continuation of your life as it has been so far—good or bad—will allow you to reflect on and understand your choices. But hey! For those of you who think that life is just fine and dandy as it is, remember that we live in an expanding universe and even the most successful, most healthy, most beautiful and happy and joyful people can still expand and grow. And those of you who don't believe that you can change your lives, or maybe you are in denial that a change is needed—please—do take the journey of writing the Probable Scenario. It will surprise you! By the simple fact of writing this scenario you will grow in consciousness and this expanded consciousness will uplift your life. Either way, writing down the Probable Scenario—whether you want to continue to live the life that you live or you want to begin to make changes—is like looking at yourself and your life in the mirror. You will begin to see your personal myth.

So now to the drawing board! Answer the questions in writing under the heading "Scenario A: The Probable Scenario." You can write in the present or future tense, and you can combine both. Let your imagination and creativity flow. Let yourself be guided by your intuition, and trust your inner voice that will sometimes speak in very specific terms and at other times will be more general. This goes for all three scenarios. Most importantly, enjoy the process!

The artist Michelangelo said: "Every block of stone has a statue inside it and it is the task of the sculptor to discover it. The greater danger for most of us lies not in setting our aim too high and falling short, but in setting our aim too low, and achieving our mark."

In writing the scenarios—which is the heart of Way Ahead—you are sculpting your life. So let yourself dream and imagine, envision, meditate and pray—and ask for what you want and need. Take off the block of stone encasing your life and discover the "you," you have been destined to be.

To view yourself from the widest perspective, draw a Mind Map. The illustration is an example. Use color, be creative, make your own. One of my friends purchases sheets of large paper from the 99 Cents Only Store and draws huge maps for the coming years. Write down the areas in your life in which you spend the most time and energy in. These are the areas that are most important to you. These can be personal, professional, financial, spiritual, creative or political. For example: Marriage and children (personal), writing books and publishing (professional), real estate (financial), yoga and tai-chi (spiritual), water color drawing class (creative), Human Rights advocacy (political).

You can add new fields of interest—things you've always wanted to do and now the time has come. Follow your love and your passion as you fill in the Mind Map. Trust yourself and believe your intuition. As Joseph Campbell always said:

**Follow Your Bliss**

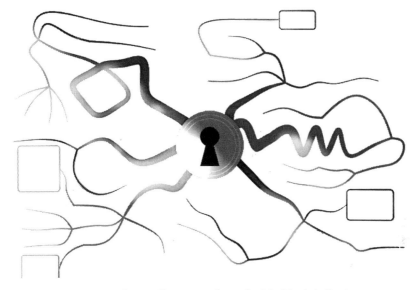

*Figure 8: Mind map illustration from the M. Glock collection.*

**Now that you have your Mind Map, look back at your life and answer these questions·**

- What were your highest aspirations in childhood and adolescence?

- What were your talents? Your gifts?

- What motivated you? Was it your parents? A schoolteacher? A public figure like John Kennedy, for example, or Martin Luther King, or the physicist and chemist Madame Currie, or a book by Maya Angelou?

- Acknowledge times in your life when you were happy and fulfilled; then recognize the times that left you bereft and desperate.

- What were your biggest challenges?

- Remember some of your night dreams and synchronicities.

## Now look at your life today

- Have your aspirations and hopes been realized? Try to understand why. Those that have not yet been realized—try to understand why. Imagine realizing these in the future.

- Did your dreams foreshadow your future in some way? Look back in retrospect: did you consciously or unconsciously follow any of them? It's not too late to start to pay attention to your dreams and to follow them... even those dreams you've had long ago and paid no attention to.

- Have your talents been utilized? And those talents that are still dormant—can you kindle a fire underneath them so they could be realized?

Let us take the example of a dream Albert Einstein dreamed in his youth:

"I was sledding with my friends at night. I
started to slide down the hill but my sled
started going faster and faster. I was going
so fast that I realized I was approaching the
speed of light. I looked up at that point
and I saw the stars. They were being
refracted into colors I had never seen before.
I was filled with a sense of awe. I
understood in some way that I was looking at
the most important meaning in my life."

Looking back at this dream near the end of his life, Einstein said, "I knew I had to understand that dream and you could say, and I would say, that my entire scientific career has been a meditation on my dream." Later in life Albert Einstein had more dreams that led him to discover and develop the Theory of Relativity.

In one dream, he was sledding down a
mountain in an ever-increasing speed
until he noticed the stars looked different
because of his speed. In another dream
he saw a farmer who had an electric fence
around a pasture where cows were standing.

## As soon as the farmer turned on the electric fence, the cows jumped away from the fence one by one in a wave motion.

From these dreams, Einstein realized that things appear differently to different people depending on the place they were standing—due to the time it takes for light to reach them.

I am inspired by Carl Jung and believe, as he postulated, that our unconscious will give us dreams in which the trajectory and meaning of our lives will be suggested, even revealed, if only we were wise enough to decode them and courageous enough to follow them. I will briefly describe the life path of a friend of mine to demonstrate Scenario A, B, and C. Today my friend is a meditation teacher and peace activist but it has not always been the case. Here is part 1 of her story.

As a child she was a joyful, talented, easygoing child, who loved to help people and bring joy to everyone she met. But in adolescence, with the unexpected twists and turns of life, she fell into a depression, inherited from her mother and grandmother. The world darkened around her, she lost purpose and direction, and the only thing that eased her pain was smoking marijuana. She was not a junky. She worked in the film industry by day and only smoked marijuana at night, as many of her generation were in the habit of doing. But the depression and her sense of worthlessness and lack of direction only intensified. One day someone took her to a meditation program. That night she had a dream. In the dream she entered a dark room and turned on the light. She was happy and laughing in this room like the child she had once been. When it was time to leave the room, she went to turn off the light but no light switch would turn the light off! She woke up from the dream with a feeling of awe and expansion. But at night she smoked marijuana again. And continued to be miserable and depressed. She told herself that it had been only a dream and had no significant value or relationship to her depression.

This is Scenario A. Even though we get a hint that things could be different and better, we continue to ride the wave of inertia, of hopelessness and denial, unable to make any positive change in our lives....

**Scenario A is your mirror! Look deeply into it with acceptance and self-respect, and decide what changes you want to make, and can make. Trust and go for it!**

- Write your biography: artistic, economic and spiritual.

- Write the history of your relationships. Connect the dots.

- What were the best things you did?

- What were the worst ones?

- What feedback did you receive in either situation?

### Scenario B· The Preferable (your best hopes)

This scenario is 180 degrees opposite to the Probable Scenario, and describes what will happen when we take Albert Einstein's advice and solve the problem with a different consciousness than the one that created it.

This is the scenario we all wish for and fantasize about: world peace, justice and freedom across the planet, a sustainable environment, and in personal matters, a million dollars in the bank, eternal youth, brilliant health, beauty, love, talent, success and fame.

As in the metaphor of the field, so in Scenario B, we plant seeds that have never been planted in this plot of land or anywhere else before, and when these seeds grow, they become the super-food plant of the future that solves world hunger, brings peace on earth, heals cancer and all mental illnesses known to women and men. Is all of this preferable? Yes. Realistic? No. But worth fantasizing about, hoping for, wishing for, and even considering—for as the saying goes, when we shoot for the moon, if we fall, we fall among the stars.

So how does one proceed from Scenario A – The Probable, to Scenario B – The Preferable? Often this shift happens in a time of crisis, when fate pushes us into action.

For my friend who smoked too much marijuana for her own good, the crisis point was when she failed to honor an appointment to help someone with a serious matter because she was too high and fell asleep. She realized that if she continued to smoke marijuana on a daily basis she would never be able to help people the way she had done as a child, the way she still wished she could. At that point she remembered her dream from long ago. She felt that the dream had come to tell her something—and maybe she better listen. She suspected that underneath her depression and despair she was still that joyful, loving and adorable child. She realized that there is a light in her that cannot be extinguished, in the same way that the light in her dream could have not been turned off. She connected the dots and saw that she had that dream the night after she attended the meditation program. She went back to the meditation center. This led her to sign up for a two-year program of deep, transformational Jungian therapy. The course of study included meditation and dream analysis. She also had to write about herself, and the more she wrote the more she understood the course of events that had caused her depression and the ancestral DNA she was carrying. Bringing all this into consciousness, she slowly began to emerge from her depression. Slowly she began to reside in that room full of light—the light that cannot be extinguished—for longer and longer periods of time. At the end of the two-year program she earned a certificate as a meditation teacher and began to teach meditation to small groups of people. At the start of each meditation class she would recall her dream and center herself energetically in that room full of light, as she guided her students to go into meditation.

Now, in this state of mind, with this new consciousness, my pothead-turned-meditation-teacher friend began to work on her Scenario B. The small meditation classes she was holding were not enough. She wanted to do more. And she had yet another meaningful dream:

In the dream, she was walking down toward the beach when suddenly she heard lots of chitchat and glasses tossing, the sounds of a cocktail party. When she reached the beach and looked around, she couldn't believe it: it was a cocktail party for wild animals! Lions, elephants, tigers, wolves, zebras! The animals were seated in pairs or in small groups under umbrellas on the beach with drinks in hand, chatting and tossing their little champagne glasses. My friend said it was a vision straight out of the biblical prophecy in which, "The lion and the lamb shall lay down together." This image of peace among those who are otherwise predators inspired her Scenario B—the Preferable Scenario. She saw herself teaching meditation all over Africa and the Middle East, and envisioned these meditations healing violence and hatred and stopping war. Obviously her vision was exaggerated and her aim too high. Spreading meditation all over Africa! Yet this exaggerated vision was of value. Her belief in peace has become the cornerstone and heart of her work as a meditation teacher and peacemaker—even if her goal of flooding Africa and the Middle East with meditation has not been realized.

**Writing Scenario B· The Preferable.**

The key is to honestly explore your wild fantasies! The embryonic point of such bigness is in memory, in the imagination, in dreams you have in the night, or in all of these. This is a chance to write about fantastic ideas and impossible solutions. Amplify, exaggerate, and inflate them. Fantastically. Think about any obsessions and fascinations you have, notice how your mind latches on to a thought or an idea or image, how it repeats itself and echoes over and over again. That's your inner motor—your Daimon, your GPS—guiding you forward!

Let us be inspired by Mary Shelley, the writer of Frankenstein, allegedly the first science fiction story. One day, Shelley visited a fellow poet, Lord Byron. Byron challenged all the guests to compose a ghost story. Shelley spent several days thinking... then one night she had a dream:

"I saw the pale student of unhallowed arts kneeling beside the thing he had put together. I saw the hideous phantasm of a man stretched out, and then, on the working of some powerful engine, show signs of life and stir with an uneasy, half vital motion. Frightful must it be; for supremely frightful would be the effect of any human endeavor to mock the stupendous mechanism of the Creator of the World."

And so came to life Frankenstein....

To write Scenario B, recall a moment of success in your life, a meaningful dream you had in the night, a synchronicity, or a vision that came to you in a moment of inspiration. Then exaggerate it a thousand times. For example:

- If you acted in a scene in an acting class and got a standing ovation, write in your scenario that you are receiving the Oscar for best leading woman or man in a film.

- If you have a lovely little apartment in the West Village in New York, imagine yourself owning a duplex penthouse on Park Avenue with a private pool and Jacuzzi.

- If you just released fifteen pounds on a juicing diet, imagine yourself loosing fifty pounds and wearing the clothes' size you wore before you gave birth to three children.

- If defending your PhD was a success, imagine your dissertation is a New York Times best seller, winning the Pulitzer Prize, and is translated into eighteen languages, selling millions, and influencing readers across the world that love is the answer.

- If you helped one child in a war zone get an education, imagine you are one of the UN ambassadors advocating and founding free and excellent education for all children in all countries from kindergarten through college.

- If you healed one person with energy healing such as Reiki or White Light, imagine yourself establishing such kind and tender yet powerful healing modalities in all hospitals across the US and Canada.

- If you had a dream that came true, imagine another dream you had, one that seems unbelievable, farfetched wishful thinking, and envision it coming to fruition.

Though most of these Preferable Scenario examples are far from being realistic, they are not pipe dreams or castles in the air. They will raise your vibration, and a higher vibrational frequency is a magnet for extraordinary things to manifest in your life and in the world around you.

**Hold the highest vision for yourself and your contribution to the world. At some point in time your vision will become a reality.**

As in all scenarios, holding the Western Apache attitude is crucial. But you do not need to exert yourself, you do not need to spend sleepless nights over your scenario, or worry, or assume and speculate—will it happen? Will it not? On the contrary! The more peaceful your mind is, the more relaxed and healthy your body, the higher your frequency will resonate. Jalaludin Rumi is sitting in his own place of patience when he tells us:

**"When I run after what I think I want, my days are a furnace of stress and anxiety; if I sit in my own place of patience, what I need flows to me, and without pain. From this I understand that what I want also wants me, is looking for me and attracting me. There is a great secret here for anyone who can grasp it."**

Chemist August Kekule's dream that led him to the discovery of benzene (C6H6) is most appropriate and inspiring in context of Scenario B:

It started with an image of atoms dancing. Gradually the rhythm of the dancing atoms changed and turned into a group of snakes swallowing their tails. After waking up and drawing the images down, Kekule literally discovered before his eyes a seemingly impossible chemical structure! It was benzene (C6H6) and the drawing was in the shape of a "ring."

*Figure 9: Modified image From Wellcome Library, London: Cyprianus, M. L., Clavis Inferni sive magia alba et nigra approbata Metratona. Published: 18th century.*

August Kekule was the principal founder of the theory of chemical structure. His mind was constantly constructing and deconstructing chemical formulas and their use to the advancement of humankind. His unconscious was working behind the scenes of his conscious mind and offered him this prophetically scientific dream. We would not have cars, planes and trains today if it were not for benzene—the 6-sided model that was foreshadowed in August Kekule's dream, a dream he followed to its end conclusion.

When writing Scenario B—the Preferable Scenario—dream big, aim high, and write it down. With detail! It is a way to invite your unconscious to cooperate with you—to bring you dreams and synchronicities that will assist you in reaching your goals. You are not alone! Your unconscious is there to lead and to guide you. Trust it!

If Scenario A—the Probable—is a mirror of your life today, and Scenario B is your ideal, utopic life that may not be achievable today but expresses who you could be in your utmost potential in an utmost world—what then is Scenario C? The alchemical marriage between the two!

## Scenario C: The Possible

And it is indeed possible, that something in between! We combine the above two scenarios—the one we know how to do and are good at but has not made us happy and satisfied, (or, agreeably, can improve even a satisfied life), with the scenario which is our highest and mightiest ideal that would benefit ourselves and the world if only it weren't that risky and probably impossible and unrealistic. In combining the two, the known and the unknown, alchemy will occur—a third new kind of tree will grow—one that will contribute to us and to our surroundings at this stage of our personal and global evolution.

Beforehand we lived by chance, steered by programs that had been installed in us without our even knowing. We may have been lucky and life turned good. But now we bring this "luck" to our awareness, and in so doing, the map that has been blurred becomes crystal clear. We have a new set of glasses to see through and understand our life's journey—the old story and the new one, and how the old has given birth to the new. This map can guide us onward as well as inspire other people.

The story of my friend, the meditation teacher, will illuminate and describe Scenario C—the Possible. In Scenario A, my friend had a dream of being in a lit room whose light could not be extinguished. For years she did not believe the message in the dream and remained depressed and without direction. But in a moment of crisis, she woke up and decided to trust the dream. That was her initiation and began her journey of transformation from a depressed pothead to a meditation teacher. Once she made that decision, she was graced with a dream about peace that was so powerful it infused her with the conviction that bringing meditation to Africa and the Middle

East would heal the whole world of violence and war. This was her Scenario B. Well, as we said, it was not realistic in the first place. She couldn't possibly achieve such a gigantic goal. But it raised her vibrational frequency and gave her energy and stamina to travel to Lebanon and work with Syrian refugees. She had only fifteen or twenty students that she taught meditation and relaxation exercises to, but those few are now spreading that simple knowledge forward. This was possible, feasible, achievable, rewarding and effective. This was her Scenario C—the alchemy between Scenario A and B.

Look at your gifts, your dreams, your wishes, the people you know and the contacts you have. Look at what you wrote in Scenarios A and B, and then combine them, fuse them, and write your Scenario C. That will be POSSIBLE!

Let us be inspired by a dream of Paul McCartney that became the song "Yesterday."

**Paul McCartney composed "Yesterday" completely in his sleep. After waking up, he replicated the entire song on his piano. He translated the dream, line by line, as if someone or something else dictated it to him.**

McCartney was worried that he was plagiarizing another song-writer's work. For about a month he went around to people in the music industry and asked them if they had ever heard the song before. Eventually it became for him like handing something in to the police—"If no-one claimed it, then I could have it."

"Yesterday" has over 2200 cover versions by other renowned artists including Neil Diamond, Bob Dylan, Aretha Franklin, Marvin Gaye, Elvis Presley, Frank Sinatra and Ray Charles.

**No matter what Scenario you are writing, listen, listen, listen to your dreams! They are the call of your heart, the guidance of your old soul, so listen and act!**

To harvest the best crops, to plant the most glorious garden, you'll rely on the Jungian principles, continue to cultivate the Western Apache attitude, and write daily in your journal. You'll examine it all through the four criteria of Rene Descartes' Scientific Method, balancing your intuition, imagination and impulses with logic and analysis. If the Scientific Method helped Galileo Galilei in his magnanimous work—won't it help you?

And maybe, like Albert Einstein, you'll be lucky and find the answer to a long lost quest while riding a bicycle, doing the dishes or taking a walk...

## Before you start, and as you continue, here are additional guidelines for writing the Scenarios

At each stage ask a question such as "What is this coming to teach me?" Or, "What do I want to learn more about?" Or, "I wonder what would happen if... " Using your "research," your dreams, synchronicities, intuition and journal explorations, hypothesize! Use your imagination to answer your original question. If one of your projects is, for example, to become a parent, your question may be: how can I be a great parent? And your hypothesis may be: I will be a great parent if I am more patient, more sensitive, less stressed out, less judgmental, etc. Imagine what that would be like.

Test your hypothesis by conducting a series of experiments. You can spend time with your friend's children and see how you get along with them, where they push your buttons, and what in you needs to heal in order to be a great parent? Are you still angry at your own parents? Heal the unresolved issues in your life that may hinder on your dream of becoming a great parent.

Make careful observations and record them in our journal. Write down your feelings about the above experiences.

Analyze your findings and draw conclusions about your experiment. Was your hypothesis correct?

Share your results—your observations and conclusions—by presenting them to others; "test drive" them on colleagues, friends and family. Having done the healing work yourself, go back to the group of children you initially spent time with, and see how your experience has improved. Has it?

### As you Write the Scenarios Consider the Following:

1. How can you best isolate and articulate the key issues you want to focus on?

2. Look at the timing associated with the projects you choose. Will they take one, three or eight weeks? Will they take two, three, or seven years? Will they require learning a new skill, enrolling in higher education, participating in workshops or therapy? How will this timing affect your life in the future one, two, or five years?

3. Continue to do your depth research. Look at the complexes and constellations you are embedded in. Use the insights coming from your dreams and synchronistic events. Interview successful people and ask them what steps they took to be where they are today.

4. Choose a luminary person in the field of your choice and make him or her your inspirational figure.

5. Consider what will influence the outcome of the scenarios you are building. Some of these considerations will be practical, such as how much income you have, how much you can divert to education, or how much you can pay for a workshop to learn how to market your work. Take into consideration your

health and your commitments to family and other matters. And think of uncertainties that might act unpredictably and influence your future, such as you heath, the state of the economy, even the weather. You might need an alternate plan. As you take these considerations into account and balance them against your dreams and intentions, stories will develop and scenarios will take shape.

6.  Rehearse the implications. In real life or in your imagination, act out the outcome of each of the future worlds you're creating as if they have already come into being. This will help you refine your understanding and further enhance your vision, so you can consciously begin to live the life you choose.

Most important to remember again and again:

**Way Ahead is not a formula or a recipe but a creative adventure. The more you invest in this adventure using your body, mind and spirit, the more it will surprise you. It will end the domination of the fate you have been living within and convert your future into an authentic life you have fashioned and designed.**

# CHAPTER TEN
# MY THREE SCENARIOS

*"Do you wait for things to happen, or do you make them*

*happen yourself? I believe in writing your own story."*

~ *Charlotte Eriksson*

*"We have more control than most of us realize. Each day is filled with*

*thousands of opportunities to change the story of our lives."*

~ *Michael Hyatt, bestselling author and life coach*

In this chapter I will share with you my own Way Ahead, and the three scenarios for my future life that I wrote in 2007. I will share my research in preparation for writing the scenarios, my experience of maintaining the Apache Mind attitude throughout the process, as well as sections from my journals, and how I evaluated it all against Descartes' Scientific Method.

## The Research· Reflection on my Past Successes and Failures

In 2006 I finished and defended my Ph.D. that described the three
scenarios in which I perceived how America would unfold after the
9/11 terrorist attacks (described in the introduction to this book.)
At that time I was living in a loft on Pico Blvd. in Santa Monica,
CA, close to the Pacific Ocean. I had a digital media agency focused
on branding, marketing and interactive web design. But I was in a
state of personal and professional transition. When I looked back
at my life I saw that I had been engaged in many professional fields,
only to find myself at some point deeply dissatisfied and searching
for the next adventurous endeavor. Each such dissatisfaction was
a crossroads in which I had to leave the past behind and find a
new path forward.

I had started out as a telephone technician with the New Zealand
Post office in Wellington. But I was soon dissatisfied with my work
and extended my education into advanced mathematics, ending up
in charge of the telecommunications in and out of New Zealand's
"White house," and moving up to train technicians in installing the
country's digitized communication network. Dissatisfied with that,
I enrolled in interior design school in Auckland, 400 miles away,
leaving my hometown for good, and earning a Bachelor's degree
in interior design and a Master in environmental design. For my
final year project I designed and executed the interior of a fashion
house. It was a professional project and not the final exam set by
the school. It took some convincing on my part for the school to
give me my degrees. I was in my early 20's when I opened "Design
Design," a 3000 sq. foot retail store that packaged up and sold
creative artifacts for the home, Pottery Barn style, before Pottery
Barn in the United States began to manufacture similar items.
Simultaneously I ran a design studio and a manufacturing company

that marketed and delivered products to other design stores in New Zealand and Australia. My first real estate project was a run down house in Herne Bay in Auckland. I tore it down, and with my father rebuilt it from the ground up. He became angry when I had incorrectly measured the kitchen cabinets and he had to cut them down.


## My journal entry about that time·

"It was the last year of my father's life. I remember us sitting on the concrete steps at the end of the day's work drinking New Zealand's best Sauvignon Blanc, in a box, 'Chateau Cardboard' we called it, 'mixture of the finest years' it read on the label. It was our last project together. He died of throat cancer, having started smoking during World War II when he was a fighter pilot."

I sold the house a few years later and purchased another run down, two-story house and hired an up and coming young architect to design the first post-modern loft/house in New Zealand. The press and media loved the fresh, open, bold design and the materials: corrugated iron and colored glass. We put New Zealand's art, design and craft on the map. We were published everywhere. I became a celebrity, a designer, entrepreneur and artist with many one-man shows. A series of watercolors I presented was called "The OMA" series, after my grandmother who died in Casa Boba years before. But by 1986 I was dissatisfied and restless; New Zealand had become too small, I yearned to travel and explore the world. Thankfully my contacts in the government opened some doors in Tokyo for me, where I worked in the import/export business of designer goods. I collaborated, dined and partied with the most celebrated Japanese designers.

**My journal entry about that time·**

"Later that year I met a Canadian woman and she said let's travel. I loved what she said, and at Maxim's in Paris I asked her to marry me. We immigrated to the US in 1988. I had several one-man shows at top galleries on Melrose Avenue in Los Angeles. We started a couture babywear line with celebrity clients including Rod Stewart and his wife. We were selling on the Sunset Strip, living in Beachwood Canyon under the Hollywood sign, and we were miserable. The Marriage lasted eighteen months. After she left, my dog Wellington and I spent a lot of time walking the Santa Monica Mountains and the 4,300 acres of Griffith Park. I always loved nature, these walks were a respite from life, from business, from relationships."

But my heart was empty. I threw myself into work and became the creative director for various media companies. With one company we pooled marketing dollars from AT&T and Cisco, and created campaigns with full-page color images of what the Internet would soon look like for America, for the world. Our ads showed people of all races and ethnicities using smart phones, social media, and signing business contracts online. We visualized the Internet delivering High Definition movies to the home and on fast mobile phones, and predicted the demise of movie theatres. We began making commercials to lure the American people into buying the products and technology the big companies were marketing on the Internet. We bought hundreds of thousands of dollars worth of editing equipment: Avids, monitors, computers, and high-speed drives. But we missed the wave. We watched our business be decimated when Apple released Final Cut Pro, software that accomplishes the same job as Avid at a fraction of the cost. We ended up with great debt while kids out of film school were making a fortune cutting national commercials on their laptops.

Once again I was unhappy, dissatisfied and at a crossroads. When the gates of Pacifica opened for me and I began a Ph.D. program in philosophy with an emphasis in Depth Psychology, the gates to my true calling opened too. I was like a dog with a bone. I couldn't let go. I felt something. Something I had always searched for was coming closer. I had always said I was a futurist. I read nothing other than science fiction when I lived in New Zealand. I had always longed for "elsewhere." I had lived in New Zealand, Tokyo, Italy, Paris and Los Angeles. I was a designer, building models of ideas, and showing people my sketches of what could exist tomorrow. Now at Pacifica, my outward journeys switched to inward ones. My Ph.D. program was the place where my inward journeys informed and inspired the outward ones—primarily my Cultural Futuristics dissertation.

## My journal entry about that time·

"Philosophy is Anima work. Philosophy means you are a 'lover of wisdom" as Philo means lover and Sopher comes from Sophia, the goddess of wisdom. Carl Jung said, "The Anima is a personification of all feminine tendencies in a man's psyche..." Anima work is feminine work, a poetics that requires the soul of reverie and remembering. The feminine, therefore, must be securely placed and honored for the imagination to be unleashed. Her name is Sophia, a trusted ally and guide. I'll call my imagination by name, Sophia. A necessary and most vital ingredient I say, if humanity is to successfully integrate psychoanalysis for the sake of the survival of humanity."

Through the research stage of reflecting on my successes and failures in life, I held and maintained the Western Apache's state of mindfulness. I meditated daily and took walks in nature. I wrote daily in my journal. I applied Descartes' Scientific Method. I questioned my motives and contemplated whether my successes and failures were a result of pure luck or hard work. I broke every area in my life into smaller sections to understand how issues were connected to other ones. I learned how to solve the simplest problems first, and I was thorough in my self-inquiry and examination of all elements in my research. Now came the time to write the three scenarios for my future.

## My Scenario A – The Probable

The Mirror: what my life looks like these days, and how it will probably continue if I don't make any substantial changes in consciousness, in my attitude, and in my habits.

It is 2007 and I've just finished my Ph.D. I'm depleted of energy, exhausted from reading and writing. I don't want to touch a book for years to come. I want to move away, start something new, or not, I don't know. To pay my way through graduate school I had built a digital marketing agency and was getting into designing, deploying and marketing websites. I'll focus on that. But I am also a man. I've spent the last five years in my head. I want to get out, get about. Happy hour at Chaya on Main Street in Santa Monica, here I come.

Over Sushi and Sapporo I read the local Venice magazine and saw a new building of lofts for sale in Marina del Rey. I calculated my rent over the last seven years, $2750 per month, times 84 months. Yikes, I should buy a place; at least it will go up in value! The following morning I do, with $10,000 down and a Countrywide loan. New place, 1900 sq. feet, empty. But, I will have a first and second mortgage, I need to grow the business, so let me throw myself into work. The place is empty, too big for me, it is time for a relationship, time for Match.com. I found her. She responded, and we remembered that we had talked two years before on Match but I didn't hear from her again.

"I thought you were a playboy," she now explained. I told her that I was not. I told her about my Ph.D. in philosophy and the book I had written, Raisin Bread Toast, about my exploits. "I am a storyteller, it is my craft." She didn't believe me but I asked her to marry me and we did. She had a nine-year old daughter, and having a family was attractive. We remodeled the loft and got into business together. My wife had been selling promotional tools and services to lawyers. We upgraded our business, building websites for lawyers and optimizing their marketing. I felt a great loss over abandoning my dissertation and my idea to build a Think Tank that uses the methodology I had invented in my Ph.D. But we needed money to pay for the loft, the marriage, life. The business will grow rapidly, I thought. It will be like Jack and the Bean Stalk or the Golden Goose. A couple of glasses of wine every night will help me cope with the stress of working all day.

While doing my Ph.D., I had discovered that I am mostly what Carl Jung called an "introvert." I am sensitive, I like to think, feel, write, be alone with my art, meditate, write down my dreams, take long contemplative walks, and listen to my intuition. I am at my best when visualizing and creating big projects, not at my best when having to manage the minutiae, more trivial details that any business or creative endeavor also requires. But now I must push through all of that and be practical, logical and realistic, as if my graduate degree is in business administration and not in philosophy. I have to hire independent contractors, train and supervise them, write their checks, keep track of expenses and accounting, and plan for inevitable catastrophic failures and hackers. None of this is the strength of the introvert. But I am a smart boy and I will do it. I quickly master the evolving world of servers, protocols, search engines optimizing (SEO), website design and web hosting. I suppress my needs and throw myself into my work.

Not fitting in this world of doing, making, running, producing and scheduling, I become disheartened and depressed, but still, I give it my best shot. After three years, the stress will have sunk its teeth deeply into my neck. To cope with the depression, I will be drinking too much. I will not be walking in the hills and mountains the way I used to with my dog Wellington. The economy seems to have grown but the Republicans in power have not created any new direction or posed a vision for the future. Not like John F. Kennedy and landing Americans on the moon before anyone else. It's 2007, and I can feel the real estate bubble we are in is going to crash and I will lose my loft. But I am strong and smart, I'll figure out how to hold on, be a good leader, work hard, and bury my True North calling for the sake of family and home. I am a good Protestant after all. But frankly, if I continue this way, if I don't find a way back to myself, I will most probably have a stroke. I will be hospitalized and paralyzed. But I will fight to regain what I have lost. I will fight hard. Is it worth it? Do I have a choice? Can I get out of it? I don't know.

## My Scenario B – The Preferable

My Best Hopes and Dreams. This is my time to dream big and reach for the moon, for if I fall, I will fall among the stars.

As I begin to write this scenario, one night, I have a dream:

My house is a face. My face is weathered. It is a narrow house. May I enter? Yes! I enter and open the window. Dappled shafts of late afternoon sun stream in. They land on a basket filled with rolled up sacred manuscripts. I am sitting in my favorite armchair. My cat is asleep, stretched out with his paws curled on top of my unfinished poetry. I smell the Russian Caravan tea steeping in the teapot. The tea smell mingles with the rich earth smell of the forest outside. All is so calm and serene. I am calm and serene.

"Thank you," I say. "May I be gifted with an object?"

I hear a faint answer.

"Yes. You may have one of the black crow's feathers from the Botswana basket."

I awake with a sense of awe and direction. According to Native American tradition, crow is the wisest bird and a crow's feather represents a major change on the horizon. I am filled with hope and immediately know what this change must be.

I must learn to balance the two main aspects of my personality: the introvert and the extrovert.

And so I will do. I will utilize my expertise in design and high tech and build a great company brand with new and exiting products. I will build it while maintaining the calm and stillness I felt in the dream. I will manage my work and my personal wellbeing while drinking tea rather than alcohol. I will create HD and broadband for mobile phones, and design gorgeous and fast fetish objects that you just cradle, touch and turn. With SMS and text messaging as the new killer application, I will create educational programming and Do It Yourself videos that teach how to do anything. With everything becoming freely available online, I will champion an open source and end the tyranny of closed, expensive systems that require licenses and teams of specialists to fix things when they go awry. My company will produce a final payout of multi-millions. With parts of the funds I will design and establish a successful, one of a kind, bed and breakfast in Vermont.

Working on my Ph.D. entrusted me with a body of knowledge that I now want to share, especially with men, who, to some degree and in many circles, have been deprived of the experience of inner spiritual growth. I found a men's group of seasoned Los Angeles professionals, a group that includes CEOs, a Rabbi, entertainment lawyers, actors and entrepreneurs. I begin to fit into my own shoes of CEO, leader, philanthropist, venture capitalist. I mentor startup visionaries and build an incubation environment for emerging talent. Eventually Silicon Valley realizes that all the creative people live in Silicon Beach—a name coined for Santa Monica, Venice and Marina del Rey in Southern California. Technology is important, but "Content is King!" What we write, how the pages are designed, and how they are delivered to the user will make or break a business. That's what I'll do all day—think in storytelling terms and narrative structures, and seek great visuals and how to best communicate them. Since I live by the ocean, on my lunch breaks I'll go surfing in the sea...

## Journal entry while writing Scenario B·

"My stepdaughter studies and excels in a Waldorf education school. She is beautiful, smart, wise, and a little bit sassy. My life with my American wife is blossoming into a relationship that balances family union, work, creativity and community participation. We hold great dinner parties that are more like salons of intellectual explorations."

## Another Journal entry·

"I pick up reading again. I must read, a lot, everything, as I am the chair of an International Jungian association that is open to professionals of other disciplines, artists, cultural innovators, designers, writers, and of course analysts, psychotherapists, and Jungian scholars. I am the head of international conferences. I travel and speak at universities and centers worldwide, like the University of Zurich in Switzerland, Yale and Cornell in the US, and the Center of the Book in Cape Town, South Africa. I visit Carl Jung's house on Lake Zurich. I rent a room in a hotel by the lake and write my autobiography from a Jungian perspective. I take walks in the woods and swim in the cool lake to ignite my inspiration and my own way of communing with Carl Jung."

As I write Scenario B, more and more ideas are coming to me ... and I must write them down. It's a way of paving a path toward the moon. I will investigate and write about natural and man-made disasters, and give deep thought and contemplation to the connection between ethics and morality and geopolitical events. I will invent several more methods that use the methodologies I mashed together in my Ph.D. dissertation, but for different purposes and focused on different subject matters. One of them will be a process to forecast the future using films. I'll title it Film Futuristics. Another will be a process for individuals to design their own future, outlined and explored in a book titled Your Future in Plain Sight. I will build a membership website so that readers can join a tribe to work the process, and I'll hire the best marketing directors to advertise my work worldwide.

With a heart overflowing with love, I will teach monthly workshops based on the book and offer scholarships to serious individuals who want to discover themselves and transform their lives and our world. I will be known as a teacher, academic, intellectual, thinker, explorer and futurist working to contribute to the betterment of the human condition. I will do this within four years from now. The project will be out in the world in 2011.

### From my journal·

"With strong writing muscle, I turn to writing a science fiction novel, titled The Modern Martian and the Soul. It's a philosophical tale set on Mars after artificial intelligence has surpassed the human brain. In a barren landscape where humans have transcended biology, achieved greater computational capacity than their minds and mastered immortality, a man and a woman realize they have lost the ability to dream, to connect with their unconscious and instincts. Desperate, they journey in search of their souls."

The book will win the Pulitzer Prize and will be on the New York Times bestseller list for two years. Warner Brothers will buy the rights to the book and hire James Cameron to write the script and direct the film. On the first weekend, the film will earn two hundred million at the box office, doubling its investment, as it is a masterpiece of stunning visuals and archetypal characters. It plays right into the most primal human need, the assurance that no matter what, the soul will always be mightier than any machine. It is a classic that for generations to come will be remembered and studied.

My other two books are published by the international academic publishing house, Taylor & Francis. The first is titled A Brief History of the Future, and is an overview of mankind's longing to know the future and how futuristics developed. It combines storytelling with the advent of new psychological and philosophical methods that infuse future planning with soul. The second book interlaces my skills as a media producer with my focus on futuristics and Carl. G. Jung's theories, investigating cultural complexes, Universal Archetypes and the Shadow. These books form the foundation for a Think Tank named Future Intelligence Agency (FIA) and weekend workshops I lead that fuse Cultural Futuristics and film, examining the influence of film on our culture. With research gained via the Think Tank I advise on film projects and work with emerging and established authors helping them deliver their expertise and authority in analog and digital formats, using great design, highly converting copywriting and marketing automation technologies.

My daily work will be well balanced with walks in nature, daily meditations, healthy nutrition, and financial support for human rights and environmental NGOs. It will also be balanced with time to rejuvenate in beautiful places and wellness retreats along with my wife.

## My Scenario C – The Possible

An alchemy between Scenario A and Scenario B. Something I can more realistically achieve.

In the late 1990s I met and spent some time with the poet David Whyte. In a poetry book of his, he wrote me a dedication:

### Dear Michael, pursue that for which you have affection.

One of my favorite poems of his is Loaves and Fishes and reflects what I have affection for, in the context of the times in which we live. We are bombarded by everything: tweets, the news, entertainment on every screen and every corner, action, adventure, always doing this and doing that, mesmerized by the fetish objects in our hands, addicted to shopping, alcohol and insatiable consumption. We are like the "hungry ghosts" in the Chinese folk story—spirits with stomachs so large they can never be full. I don't want to be like this. I want to live a peaceful life, in which my introversion feeds my outward and forward creativity.

## Loaves and Fishes
*By David Whyte*


This is not
the age of information.
This is not
the age of information.
Forget the news,
and the radio,
and the blurred screen.
This is the time of loaves
and fishes.
People are hungry,
and one good word is bread
for a thousand.


I combine and balance all the aspects of my personality to create something that makes me happy and contributes to society. I maintain the business we have and I read many books. I return to beginners' mind—open, empty and eager. I return to the Western Apache Mind—smooth, resilient and steadfast. Rather than intermittent frustrations, dissatisfactions and breakdowns I have continual, small incremental breakthroughs like in the Kaizan process.


The concept that we can design our future and live our lives from that future backwards fascinates people. When they look at those stories, those futures have become their history, and understanding how they have created their own futures is deeply empowering. We are not just cogs in a machine, we are not just feathers in the wind; we can take our own destiny by the horns and do something of our lives. It is a shift in attitude. This shift I coined Personal Future Histories. I am using my skills in technology, media and marketing to launch a campaign that markets the process of these Future Histories. I will be a successful writer, speaker, workshop leader, designer and futurist.

As I honor the sensitive, creative, artistic, more introvert side of myself, I enjoy being more alone with my own thoughts, travelling the realms of my creative imagination. In my youth I apprenticed under my father as a carpenter. I like to build things, and, like my father, I am a craftsperson. When building things one item at a time, I am in my element. I build a dining table, a bookshelf, I remodel chairs—it is such a wonderful balance to my more thinking, academic mind.

The solitary creative work allows me to connect with my moral compass. I care deeply about the world and the beings populating it. I care about building a viable ecology and a sustainable economic system where everyone—humans and non-humans—benefits. I want to think of and create a more psychologically aware democracy, and design a cohesive and conscious polis for all. I have been prepared to do this my entire life, and now is the time. I cannot do it all at once, so I will put my energy into four main areas.

1. I will design digital platforms for established and emerging authors and publish and market their books.

2. I will co-chair an international organization of Jungian studies. We will set policy, direction and tone for global membership of academics, professors, teachers and authors of Jungian related

subjects. I will design, coordinate and speak at international Jungian conferences, and work closely with multi national publishers to bring into the world other Jungian and post Jungian academic works.

3. I will write and self publish a book that inspires readers to understand, heal and upgrade their lives. I envision it selling on Amazon like hotcakes. It goes along with a workbook, weekend workshops, and interactive courseware on the Internet that I design. Maybe I will call it Way Ahead.

4. I will finally sit to write my science fiction novel, The Modern Martian and the Soul. I have been dreaming about it day and night, taking notes, researching, and now the time has come to sit and write it.

I love my Scenario C. The possible. It is a fascinating and pleasing alchemy between my birth given talents, my expertise achieved through education and experience, and my dreams and visions. It fuses all parts and aspects of me. Just thinking up and writing Scenario C has slowed me down, calmed me down. This is the scenario I choose to follow, this scenario will happen; I can feel it in my bones. It will gradually lead to the manifestation of my Scenario B—the Preferable—and my other goals. I remember my childhood dream in which I was writing at Goethe's desk, and though it has taken me over five decades, it has taken me to the real me, to sit and write to you from my own desk. It is my wish for you that you follow your deepest dreams, and you find your own "desks."

# ADIEU, GOODBYE AND GOODSPEED

*"Each Day of Our Lives We Make Deposits in the*

*Memory Banks of Our Children."*

*~ Charles R. Swindoll*

## The Time Before Death
*A Poem by the 15th Century Indian Mystic Kabir*
*Translated by Robert Bly*

Friend? Hope for the Guest while you are alive.

Jump into experience while you are alive!

Think... and think... while you are alive.

What you call "salvation" belongs to the time before death.

If you don't break your ropes while you're alive,

do you think ghosts will do it after?

The idea that the soul will join with the ecstatic

just because the body is rotten –

that is all fantasy.

What is found now is found then.

If you find nothing now,

you will simply end up with an apartment in the

City of Death.

If you make love with the divine now, in the next

life you will have the face of satisfied desire.

So plunge into the truth, find out who the Teacher is,

Believe in the Great Sound!

Kabir says this: When the Guest is being searched for,

it is the intensity of the longing for the Guest

that does all the work.

Look at me, and you will see a slave of that intensity.

"The Whole future of the earth depends on

awakening our faith in the future."

~ Pierre Teilhard, 1963.

# NOTES

Way Ahead is more than a book to read, it is a program for life. It is designed to be a workbook that you can use to design your future. Make notes here about your rebirth and renewal journey and the insights you glean along the way and most importantly, write down your dreams from the night. Ultimately, it is these pages of your own work that will outshine what has been written elsewhere.

A large size workbook and journal are available as companion tools to Way Ahead as well as online program(s)—available at www.WayAhead. work

The books are available globally from Amazon.com.

# Connect

Michael Glock Ph.D., is a futurist, digital media architect and platform expert. After gaining his doctorate in philosophy, he furthered his research by developing methodologies for Future Studies & Scenario Planning for the public & private sphere. He has developed concepts and systems and written books such as Cultural and Film Futuristics, Way Forward Engineering, DestinyOS and Way Ahead and is a former co-chair of the International Association for Jungian Studies (IAJS). He is the co-editor of *Jungian Perspective on Rebirth and Renewal: Phoenix Rising* published in December 2016 by Routledge, London England.

♦ Learn more about Way Ahead Programs. Become a tribe member at www.WayAhead.work

♦ Find out about weekend and scheduled workshop retreats
♦ Schedule a session with Dr Glock
♦ Facebook: facebook.com/DrMichaelGlock
♦ LinkedIn: linkedin.com/in/drmichaelglock
♦ Visit Dr Glock on Twitter: @DrMichaelGlock
♦ Visit Dr Glock on Google+: +DrMichaelGlock
♦ For Way Forward Engineering, visit DrMichael Glock.com

Change and shifts will always be a part of life. Follow me and become a member of a group that cares deeply about the future.

Nameste

Made in the USA
San Bernardino, CA
04 June 2018